Article 33

Protection from Narcotic
Drugs and Psychotropic Substances

The titles published in this series are listed at brill.nl/cunc

A Commentary on the United Nations Convention
on the Rights of the Child

Editors

André Alen, Johan Vande Lanotte, Eugeen Verhellen,
Fiona Ang, Eva Berghmans, Mieke Verheyde, and Bruce Abramson

Article 33

Protection from Narcotic Drugs
and Psychotropic Substances

By

Damon Barrett and Philip E. Veerman
With a foreword by Dr. Dainius Puras

MARTINUS
NIJHOFF
PUBLISHERS

LEIDEN • BOSTON
2012

Cover illustration: Naida, 1½ years old.

This book is printed on acid-free paper.

Library of Congress Cataloging-in-Publication Data

Barrett, Damon.
  Article 33 : protection from narcotic drugs and psychotropic substances / by Damon
Barrett and Philip E. Veerman ; with a foreword by Dainius Puras.
    p. cm. – (A commentary on the United Nations Convention on the Rights of the Child,
ISSN 1574-8626)
    ISBN 978-90-04-14732-4 (pbk. : alk. paper) 1. Children—Drug use. 2. Children—Substance
use. 3. Children (International law) 4. Children—Legal status, laws, etc. 5. Convention on the
Rights of the Child (1989). Article 33. 6. Substance abuse. I. Veerman, Philip E. II. Title.

  K639.B37 2012
  344.03'2290261--dc23

                                                                                    2012000217

ISSN 1574-8626
ISBN 978 90 04 14732 4 (paperback)
ISBN 978 90 04 21693 8 (e-book)

CONTENTS

LIST OF ABBREVIATIONS

ADHD	Attention-Deficit/Hyperactivity Disorder
APHA	American Public Health Association
CESCR Committee	UN Committee on Economic, Social and Cultural Rights
CND	UN Commission on Narcotic Drugs
CRC	Convention on the Rights of the Child
CRC Committee	UN Committee on the Rights of the Child
DSM-IV	Diagnostic and Statistical Manual of Mental Disorders 4th edition
FCTC	WHO Framework Convention on Tobacco Control
ICCPR	International Covenant on Civil and Political Rights
ICESCR	International Covenant on Economic Social and Cultural Rights
IDP	Internally Displaced Person
ILO	International Labour Organization
INCB	International Narcotics Control Board
IPEC	International Programme on the Elimination of Child Labour
OPAC	Optional Protocol to the Convention on the Rights of the Child on the Involvement of Children in Armed Conflict
OST	Opioid Substitution Therapy
UNAIDS	Joint United Nations Program on HIV/AIDS
UNODC	United Nations Office on Drugs and Crime
UNICEF	United Nations Children's Fund
WHO	World Health Organization

AUTHOR BIOGRAPHIES

Damon Barrett is Senior Human Rights Analyst with London-based Harm Reduction International and cofounder of the International Centre on Human Rights and Drug Policy. He is an editor-in-chief of the *International Journal on Human Rights and Drug Policy*, and editor of *Children of the Drug War: Perspectives on the Impact of Drug Policies on Young People* (IDEA, iDebate Press, New York and Amsterdam, 2011).

E mail: damon.darrett@ihra.net; damon@humanrightsanddrugs.org

Philip E. Veerman is a psychologist at Bouman mental health services in Rotterdam, where he is responsible for the professional training programme for health psychologists. He is an independent expert of the courts in the Netherlands.

E mail: p.veerman@boumanggz.nl; info@drpveerman.nl

TEXT OF ARTICLE 33

ARTICLE 33

States parties shall take all appropriate measures, including legislative, administrative, social and educational measures, to protect children from illicit use of narcotic drugs and psychotropic substances as defined in the relevant international treaties and to prevent the use of children in the illicit production and trafficking of such substances.

ARTICLE 33

Les États parties prennent toutes les mesures appropriées, y compris des mesures législatives, administratives, sociales et éducatives, pour protéger les enfants contre l'usage illicite de stupéfiants et de substances psychotropes, tels que les définissent les conventions internationales pertinentes, et pour empêcher que des enfants ne soient utilisés pour la production et le trafic illicites de ces substances.

FOREWORD

Dr. Dainius Puras
Member of the UN Committee on the Rights of the Child, 2007–2011

The UN Convention on the Rights of the Child (CRC) remains one of the most widely ratified of all instruments of international law. Its influence is clear in many countries around the world, from law reform to the significant increases in national commissioners for children basing their work on its many protections. Indeed, one of the main strengths of the CRC is that it is comprehensive, covering civil and political rights, economic, social and cultural rights, and a number of rights unique to children and unique to this historic document, including the right of the child to be heard and have his or her views taken into account.

Unfortunately, that strength has its risks, one of which being that some articles do not receive the attention they deserve. These include, for example, the right to play (article 31), or the child's right to freedom of association (article 15). To my mind, however, and in my experience, the clearest example, and one of considerable importance, is article 33—protection from narcotic drugs and psychotropic substances.

This is not to say that children are absent from debates around drugs and the drug trade. Certainly not. Children are at the forefront of such debates, but the rights of the child are not—a staggering omission given the global nature of the drugs question, the influence of drug policies on children and young people, and given that drugs are specifically referred to in the CRC, unique among the UN human rights treaties.

Article 33 is broadly framed and needs closer attention. It demands a child rights based response, but it is extremely rare to see national policies on drugs referring to the CRC, never mind basing their provisions on it. In addition, there is a lack of international guidance on child rights based responses to drug use, drug related harm and the drug trade. We see little in the way of clear guidelines from UNICEF, the UN Office on Drugs and Crime and other agencies. International resolutions on these issues are not sufficient in detail.

The Committee on the Rights of the Child, of course, has an important role in this. Article 33 of the CRC demands it. But with such a wide ranging mandate and with drugs being such a huge and complex issue, the Concluding

Observations of the Committee have been limited. Information from States parties has been useful but without significant input from civil society, it is difficult to get a handle on the situation on the ground. The Committee has yet to develop a General Comment on article 33, an oversight requiring urgent attention in my view. During my term on the Committee I worked to improve our commentaries on drugs, and with a number of Concluding Observations I believe we made important progress. But far more needs to be done by the Committee, by civil society and by national authorities to understand and begin to develop child rights based drug policies. It is, after all, a legal obligation.

For twenty-first century children drugs are becoming an increasingly prominent aspect of growing up. I know this from my day to day work with young people who use drugs. For some, drug dependence, either their own or within their families, is a source of significant harm. For policy makers and those in positions of power, drug control poses one of the key policy dilemmas of this generation. This commentary is an important contribution to international and national debates around children and drug policies. It considers article 33 within the broader framework of the CRC, with detailed commentary on the subject matter the article covers—drug use and the drug trade. It also considers other aspects of international law, including the three core international drug conventions and the WHO Framework Convention on Tobacco Control. With this commentary, Barrett and Veerman have provided a detailed window into the many ways in which the CRC, via article 33, may influence our thinking on drug policies. I urge students, academics, Committee members, UN staff and national policy makers with an interest in drugs and the rights of the child to read it and join in this discussion of such fundamental importance to the world's children.

CHAPTER ONE

INTRODUCTION*

1. Drugs and the CRC: A Neglected Issue

1. The Convention on the Rights of the Child is the only core United Nations human rights treaty to specifically refer to drug use and the drug trade. Article 33 is generally framed and compact: *'States parties shall take all appropriate measures, including legislative, administrative, social and educational measures, to protect children from the illicit use of narcotic drugs and psychotropic substances as defined in the relevant international treaties and to prevent the use of children in the illicit production and trafficking of such substances'.*[1] It is unique in the UN human rights framework and unusual in a legal and policy environment within which human rights and drug policy have developed in 'parallel universes',[2] 'practically detached' from each other in the UN system[3] and in national laws and policies.

2. Human rights are all but absent from the three main UN treaties that form the backbone of drug control internationally: the Single Convention on Narcotic Drugs 1961 (as amended by the 1972 Protocol on the Single Convention), the Convention on Psychotropic Substances 1971, and the Convention Against the Illicit Traffic in Narcotic Drugs and Psychotropic Substances 1988.[4] The phrase 'human rights' appears explicitly only once in over one hundred articles in these treaties, drafted and adopted over four decades, all in the era of the post war modern human rights movement. The General Assembly asserts and reasserts in its annual omnibus resolution on

---

* September 2011.

[1] Convention on the Rights of the Child, G.A. res. 44/25, annex, 44 U.N. GAOR Supp. (No. 49) at 167, U.N. Doc. A/44/49 (1989), entered into force Sept. 2, 1990.

[2] P. Hunt, 'Human Rights, Health and Harm Reduction: States' Amnesia and Parallel Universes', Rolleston Oration, 19th International Harm Reduction Conference, Barcelona, 11 May 2008.

[3] Report of the Special Rapporteur on torture and other cruel, inhuman or degrading treatment or punishment, Manfred Nowak, (UN Doc No A/HRC/10/44, 2009), para. 51.

[4] Single Convention on Narcotic Drugs, 1961, March 30, 1961, 520 U.N.T.S. 204; Protocol Amending the Single Convention on Narcotic Drugs, 25 March 1972, T.I.A.S No 8118, 976 UNTS 3; Convention on Psychotropic Substances, 1971 32 U.S.T. 543, T.I.A.S. 9725, 1019 U.N.T.S. 175; Convention Against the Illicit Traffic in Narcotic Drugs and Psychotropic Substances 1988, U.N. Doc. E/CONF.82/15 (1988), reprinted in 28 I.L.M. 493.

the issue that 'countering the world drug problem' must be carried out in full conformity with the UN Charter and fundamental human rights.[5] But it has never requested a study by any mechanism into whether this in fact happens or on the impacts of drug control on human rights. Drug control has never been a thematic debate at the Human Rights Council (or the former Commission), and human rights has never been a thematic debate at the UN Commission on Narcotic Drugs (CND).[6] Drugs and drug control are absent from the UN Charter and absent from almost every UN human rights treaty or declaration.

3. The discourse has, in recent years, improved significantly due to the efforts of various civil society organisations and key individuals. Some UN member states have also sought to bring human rights more to the forefront of drug policies internationally, in particular those within Latin America and the European Union.[7] More and more, issues related to drug use and the drug trade, and, importantly, the laws and policies put in place to address these phenomena, are being passed through the lens of human rights and coming to the attention of mainstream human rights organisations and international mechanisms and monitors.[8]

4. Article 33 requires action for children in the field of drug control, and places drug policies within a complex human rights framework by nature of the very treaty within which it resides—the parallel universes of drugs and human rights brought very much together at least for children and adolescents. As a provision of international law, however, article 33 has received very little attention. Despite the relatively unique status of this article, its complex relation to other instruments of international law, its broad formulation, and the fact that it deals with a key issue of national and global

---

[5] See, for example, GA Res 63/197, 6 March 2009, para. 1; GA Res 64/192 30 March 2010, para. 2.

[6] It has been proposed by some CND member states but rejected in inter-sessional deliberations.

[7] For the debates surrounding the CND's first human rights resolution adopted in 2008 (the Commission was founded in 1946) see 'The life of a human rights resolution at the UN Commission on Narcotic Drugs' Harm Reduction International Blog, 22 April 2008 http://www.ihra.net/contents/288. Evidence of progress may be found in the fact that since the adoption of that resolution (51/12) human rights language and safeguards have become more acceptable at the Commission.

[8] See for example the Report of Anand Grover, the Special Rapporteur on the right of everyone to the enjoyment of the highest attainable standard of physical and mental health, (UN Doc No A/65/255, 2010) and the Report of Manfred Nowak, the Special Rapporteur on torture and other cruel, inhuman or degrading treatment or punishment, (UN Doc No A/HRC/10/44, 2009).

policy, very little has been published about it. Moreover, the Committee on the Rights of the Child has never held a day of general discussion on drugs or drug policies and has not adopted a General Comment on the article (various General Comments do refer to drug use, as we will see below, but none on drug trafficking). The Committee's Concluding Observations on States parties' initial and periodic reports and the 'constructive dialogues' with the delegations of States parties have been inconsistent on these issues. Some Concluding Observations have been very helpful, some either very general or a simple restatement of article 33. On occasion, the Committee's recommendations have, in our opinion, been problematic.

5. This lack of analysis on child rights and drug control is unfortunate for many reasons. Firstly, drug dependence, drug related harms and the drug trade continue to affect a wide range of child rights. Secondly, article 33 requires using the Convention on the Rights of the Child as a framework for scrutiny of policies aimed at addressing these concerns and for policy formulation moving forward. At present there is little specific to go on. Thirdly, and conversely, excessively punitive drug control laws and policies are often put in place, and human rights abuses committed, in the name of protecting children from drugs. While protecting children from drugs is at the core of article 33, it should go without saying that abusive measures to pursue that aim are not legitimate. Fourthly, the CRC is increasingly seen as justifying or bolstering the punitive status quo in drug control, rather than as a check and balance against such policies. This is despite the fact that it is well known that drug control laws and policies have created an environment within which vulnerability to human rights abuse has increased for particular vulnerable groups[9] including children. Finally, patterns of drug use and drug related harms and trends in drug trafficking have changed significantly since the drafting of the CRC. Twenty years of research into drug use and dependence, prevention, treatment and harm reduction[10] must be taken into account since its adoption, as must twenty years of experience in

---

[9] See for example, 'Making drug control fit for purpose: Building on the UNGASS decade' UN Office on Drugs and Crime, Note of the Executive Director, (No E/CN.7/2008/CRP.17, 2008) p. 11. See also C. Lloyd, 'Sinning and sinned against: The stigmatisation of problem drug users' UK Drug Policy Commission, August 2010.

[10] Harm reduction refers to policies, programmes and practices that aim to reduce the harms associated with the use of psychoactive drugs in people unable or unwilling to stop. The defining features are the focus on the prevention of harm, rather than on the prevention of drug use itself, and the focus on people who continue to use drugs. The harm reduction approach to drugs is based on a strong commitment to public health and human rights. See www.ihra.net/whatisharmreduction.

drug enforcement measures. The CRC must be able to adapt to such changing circumstances and incorporate scientific progress,[11] but the absence of
Committee guidance and academic literature on drug-related issues risks
dating the treaty and limiting its relevance.[12]

6. This commentary is intended to contribute to improving that situation.
It is not intended to provide an overview of drug use among children or
child involvement in the drug trade as many studies and reports are available elsewhere,[13] although country specific and thematic examples will be
used throughout. The Commentary instead focuses on an analysis of the text
of article 33, its relationship to other articles in the CRC and other international instruments, and provides a commentary on the normative content
of the article. In doing so, our aim is to draw broad conclusions about the
protections contained within article 33 and its interpretation given twenty-
first century circumstances.

---

[11] Article 15(1)(b) of the International Covenant on Economic Social and Cultural Rights
guarantees the right of everyone to benefit from scientific progress and its applications.

[12] On this see P. Veerman 'The ageing of the Convention on the Rights of the Child',
International Journal of Children's Rights, Volume 18, Number 4, 2010, pp. 585–618(34); and
D. Barrett and P. Veerman 'Children and drug use: the need for more clarity on State obligations in international law' *International Journal on Human Rights and Drug Policy*, Vol. I (2010)
pp. 63–81.

[13] For example, *World Drug Report 2009* (Vienna, United Nations Office on Drugs and Crime,
2009) featuring a chapter (pages 23–28) on trends in drug use among young people; C. Cook and
A. Fletcher 'Youth drug use research and the missing pieces of the puzzle: How can researchers supports the next generation of harm reduction approaches? In D. Barrett (ed.) *Children of
the Drug War: Perspectives on the Impact of Drug Policies on Young People* (New York, London and
Amsterdam, International Debate Education Association, iDebate Press, 2011) pp. 175–185;
A. Fletcher et al. 'Young people, recreational drug use and harm reduction', in *Harm reduction:
evidence, impacts and challenges* (Lisbon, EMCDDA, European Monitoring Centre for Drugs and
Drug Addiction, April 2010); Hibell B, et al. *The 2007 ESPAD* (The European School Survey on
Alcohol and other Drugs); *Substance use among students in 35 European countries*, (Stockholm,
The Swedish Council for Information on Alcohol and Other Drugs, CAN, 2009); *Young people
and injecting drug use in selected countries of Central and Eastern Europe*, (Vilnius, Eurasian Harm
Reduction Network, 2009); *Drug use and related problems among very young people (under 15 years
old)* (Lisbon, EMCDDA, 2007) L. Dowdney, *Children of the Drug Trade: a case study of children in
organised armed violence in Rio de Janeiro*, Viva Rio/ISER, 7 Letras, (2003); J. de Souza e Silva
and A. Urani, *Brazil: Children in Drug Trafficking; A Rapid Assessment*, (Geneva, ILO/IPEC, 2002);
M. Bouchard et al. 'Convenient labour: The prevalence and nature of youth involvement in
the cannabis cultivation industry' *International Journal of Drug Policy*, Vol. 20, Issue 6, pp. 467–
474; 'Alternative report to the report of the government of Colombia on the situation of the
rights of the child in Colombia', (Bogota, NGO coalition coordinated by the Coalition against
the involvement of boys, girls and youths into armed conflict in Colombia, 2005, http://www
.crin.org/docs/Colombia_COALICO_NGO_Report_EN.pdf).

2. *Children As Justification in Drug Control*

7. Children are at the forefront of political justifications for drug control measures. In the context of drug use, for example, President Nixon, launching the US 'war on drugs' said

> *Narcotics addiction is a problem which afflicts both the body and the soul of America. It comes quietly into homes and destroys children, it moves into neighbourhoods and breaks the fibre of community which makes neighbours. We must try to better understand the confusion and disillusion and despair that bring people, particularly young people, to the use of narcotics and dangerous drugs.*[14]

The preamble of the 1988 Convention Against the Illicit Traffic in Narcotic Drugs and Psychotropic Substances, meanwhile, enshrines the threat to children posed by drug trafficking in international law, expressing States parties' deep concern 'that children are used in many parts of the world as an illicit drug consumers market and for purposes of illicit production, distribution and trade in narcotic drugs and psychotropic substances, *which entails a danger of incalculable gravity*' [emphasis added].

8. Today, preambular statements in UN declarations on drugs refer to children as 'our most precious asset', framing and providing a moral basis for the policy guidance that follows.[15] Let us make no mistake, drug use among children, and the involvement of children in the drug trade are serious issues that must be addressed. The protection of children is crucial, and, indeed, there could be no better justification for drug policies. But whether the measures in fact adopted to address these concerns are justified, and whether those measures have in fact worked to protect children, are entirely different questions.

9. With this in mind, less often publicly voiced is the concern that drug control measures are increasingly having serious negative impacts on children's lives. Many punitive and abusive measures have been adopted in the name of protecting children from drugs. The Mexican government, for example, has resorted to the rhetoric of protecting children.[16] Today it is known that since

---

[14] 'Excerpts from President's Message on Drug Abuse Control', *New York Times*, (June 18, 1971) 22, http://128.91.58.209/Articles/19710618_WarOnDrugsArticle_2.PDF.

[15] Preamble, 'Political Declaration and Plan of Action on International Cooperation towards an Integrated and Balanced Strategy to Counter the World Drug Problem, adopted at the High Level Segment of the UN Commission on Narcotic Drugs', (UN Doc No E/2009/28—E/CN.7/2009/12, 2009), pp. 37–77.

[16] J. Castaneda 'What's Spanish for Quagmire? Five myths that caused the failed war next door' *Foreign Policy*, Jan/Feb 2011.

the start of the 'war on drugs' in the country over 35,000 people have been killed in the consequent violence including hundreds if not thousands of children.[17] In 2011, the Committee on the Rights of the Child (in the context of the Optional Protocol on the Involvement of Children in Armed Conflict) raised its concern 'at the high number of child victims (about 1000 dead children over the last 4 years) as a result of the fight of the army against organized crime, child rights violations and the lack of investigation of crimes perpetrated by military personnel' in Mexico.[18] As many as 50,000 children have lost at least one parent in the violence.[19] Schools and drug treatment facilities have now become targets, including numerous massacres of young people at the latter.[20] There has been a 900% increase in complaints to national human rights commissions.[21]

10. In 2009, following the passing of a new drug control bill in Indonesia, Andi Mattalatta, the Minister for Law and Human Rights, said that the new law would 'save our children and young generation.'[22] The law included the death penalty for a range of drug offences and incarceration for parents who fail to report their children's drug use, among other measures in contravention of basic rights protections.[23]

11. Mexico is currently a unique case, Indonesia less so, its approach mirrored elsewhere.[24] Less obviously problematic, however, are the majority

---

[17] According to the report 'Drug Violence in Mexico, Data and Analysis from 2001–2009' published by the Trans-Border Institute of the University of San Diego in the United States, there are no real reliable data for measuring violence related to criminal activity by drug-trafficking organizations. 'This is because such violence does not correspond to a specific legal category of criminal activity'. But it is concluded that in terms of impact, the extent to which drug-related violence (a general term relating also to 'drug violence', 'narco-violence', 'cartel-related violence', 'drug war violence', etc.) affected public officials, police, women and minors under the age of 18, was especially noticeable over the last year. See also 'Mexico's drug wars: mystery surrounds how many are dying, and who' *Guardian*, 8 December 2011, citing government figures of 35,000 dead with unofficial estimates of as high as 60,000.

[18] Committee on the Rights of the Child, *Concluding Observations: Mexico* (OPAC), (UN Doc No CRC/C/OPAC/MEX/CO/1, 2011), para. 29.

[19] Catherine Bremer, 'Special report: Mexico's growing legion of narco orphans' *Reuters*, (6 October 2010; Red por los Derechos de la Infancia en México, 'Pronunciamiento contra armas', 17 May 2010; Ruth Rodríguez, '900 menores han muerto en guerra al narco.', *El Universal*, (8 June 2010).

[20] 'Nueva matanza en un centro de rehabilitación de Ciudad Juárez', La Crónica, 17 September 2009.

[21] 'Activities Report 1999–2009', National Commission on Human Rights (CNDH).

[22] 'Indonesia's parliament enacts drugs law' *People's Daily Online*, (14 September 2009).

[23] See 'Drug addicts branded as criminals under new law' *Jakarta Post*, (15 September 2009).

[24] At the time of writing Cambodia is in the process of drafting a new law which will include detention without due process of law in drug detention centres, and includes a provision

of measures adopted to prevent drug use—education, publicity campaigns, school drug testing, criminal laws relating to use and incitement of children to use and so on. These are all adopted with the intent of protecting children from drugs. But two questions arise: have such measures in fact protected children from drugs? And have they had negative impacts on other aspects of child welfare, wellbeing and rights?

12. Studies and policy commentaries have challenged various drug prevention projects, drug treatment programmes and law enforcement strategies. But the protection of children from drugs is a strong answer, without more, to such criticism. Against this, and the inevitable sensitivities around children,[25] rational debate on drug policies is often difficult or impeded by moral panics.[26] Indeed, the very international legal system which frames and influences national polices states that 'addiction' is 'a serious evil for the individual and is fraught with social and economic danger to mankind'. It posits drug control as a moral duty to 'combat this evil'.[27]

13. Article 33 may serve as a lens through which these justifications of State drug control measures may be scrutinised; for assessing their actual impact on child rights and well being; and for articulating, as required by article 33, child rights-based responses to drug use and dependence, and to the involvement of children in the drug trade.

---

granting qualified immunity from prosecution for staff of such centres. On the conduct of these centres see *Skin on the cable: The Illegal Arrest, Arbitrary Detention and Torture of People Who Use Drugs in Cambodia* (New York, Human Rights Watch, 2010). Thirty-two jurisdictions retain the death penalty for drug offences. See P. Gallahue, *The Death Penalty for Drug Offences: Global Overview 2011*, (London, Harm Reduction International, 2011). However, only a handful carry out executions. Leading in the statistics are China, Iran, Saudi Arabia, Viet Nam, Malaysia and Singapore The Hamas government in Gaza approved in 2009 the possibility to execute drug dealers.

[25] As an example, there have been calls in recent years for people who use drugs to be sterilised in order to protect their unborn children from future abuse. See for example J. Kleeman 'Should drug addicts be sterilised?' *The Guardian*, (12 June 2010).

[26] The case of the formerly 'legal high' mephedrone in the United Kingdom serves as an example. See 'Scunthorpe parents call for mephedrone ban' *BBC News* (17 March 2010); 'Banned mephedrone cleared of blame for two deaths' *The Guardian*, (28 May 2010); 'New drug set to replace banned mephedrone as a 'legal high' *The Guardian*, (18 April 2010); P. Strange 'The new drugs taking mephedrone's place' *The Guardian* comment (2 June 2010); 'D. Nutt, Banning naphyrone will get us nowhere' *The Guardian*, Comment (9 July 2010); and 'Ivory Wave drug implicated in death of 24-year-old man' *The Guardian* (17 August 2010).

[27] Preamble, Single Convention on Narcotic Drugs 1961. See R. Lines 'Deliver us from evil: The Single Convention on Narcotic Drugs at 50' *International Journal on Human Rights and Drug Policy*, Vol. I, 2010, pp. 3–13.

3. *Article 33 in Academic Literature and Drug Policy Discourse*

14. Simply put, very little has been written in academic literature about article 33.[28] In her 1998 book on the Convention, Geraldine Van Bueren devotes just one page of text to it.[29] Guides to the *Travaux Préparatoires* take us, very helpfully, through the drafting process,[30] while Hodgkin's and Newell's Implementation Handbook of the CRC is useful to an extent in providing guidance to States parties and is intended as 'a reference in the day-to-day practical process if improving the quality of children's lives'.[31] To date, the most detailed legal analysis appears to be in Sharon Detrick's commentary on the CRC from 1999.[32] While useful, it suffers, inevitably, due to the breadth of that study, from a lack of detail about specific issues in the drugs field. Relevant NGO reports along with the voluminous literature dealing with drug use and dependence among young people and research on involvement of children in the drug trade help fill this gap, as do the many articles on, *inter alia*, HIV, street children, children in residential care, child labour, economic exploitation, juvenile justice and so on—all relevant to the topic of drugs. But even among these, putting aside a focus on article 33, there are very few articles focused on drug policy and the rights of the child—a symptom perhaps of the historical disconnect between the two fields.[33]

15. In drug policy discussions article 33 rarely arises. When it has arisen it has often been placed alongside the international drug conventions or has been limited to efforts to prevent drug use (certainly a requirement of article 33 as we will see below, but not its sole protection). Speaking at a 2010 drug conference the Swedish Minister for Health and the Elderly, Maria Larsson, framed her talk around article 33 using it to support Sweden's existing

---

[28] See, however, D. Barrett and P. Veerman o.c. (note 12).

[29] G. Van Bueren *The International Law of the Rights of the Child*, (Dordrecht, Boston, London, Martinus Nijhoff, 1998), 313–314.

[30] See for example Office of the High Commissioner for Human Rights, *Legislative History of the Convention on the Rights of the Child: Part II* (New York and Geneva, UN, 2007) and S. Detrick, *The United Nations Convention on the Rights of the Child, A Guide to the 'Travaux Préparatoires'*, (Dordrecht, Boston, London, Martinus Nijhoff, 1992).

[31] C. Bellamy, Foreword, in: R. Hodgkin and P. Newell, *Implementation Handbook for the Convention on the Rights of the Child* (New York and Geneva, UNICEF, 2002).

[32] S. Detrick *A Commentary on the United Nations Convention on the Rights of the Child* (The Hague, Martinus Nijhoff, 1998) pp. 580–587.

[33] Of note, however, is S. Gruskin, K. Plafker and A. Smith Estelle, 'Understanding and Responding to Youth Substance Use: The Contribution of a Health and Human Rights Framework' *American Journal of Public Health*, 2001: 91(12): 1954–63.

'restrictive' drug policies.[34] Of interest was the Minister's failure to mention Sweden's periodic review at the Committee on the Rights of the Child in 2009. While recognising the country's prevention measures, the Committee criticised the lack of treatment options for those under eighteen and the lack of accurate, disaggregated data on the problem in the country.[35] Less than a year later the Minister failed to refer to this when invoking article 33 to promote the Swedish Government's policies.[36] A very similar speech was delivered by the Minister in March 2011 at the 54th session of the UN Commission on Narcotic Drugs (CND),[37] the main inter-governmental body in the UN system for drug policy discussion.[38]

16. In 1999 the UN Drug Control Programme (now part of the UN Office on Drugs and Crime) presented a report to the CND entitled 'Youth and drugs: A global overview'.[39] The report failed to mention the Convention on the Rights of the Child or any aspect of human rights. A year earlier the influential 1998 Declaration on the Guiding Principles on Demand Reduction adopted at the General Assembly stated that special attention must be paid to youth.[40] It referred to the article 33 of the CRC as 'supplementary reference material'.[41]

---

[34] The speech is available online at http://vimeo.com/12228339. See also 'Swedish Action Plan on Narcotic Drugs 2006–2010' February 2008 http://www.sweden.gov.se/content/1/c6/09/88/53/49c4a92e.pdf.

[35] UN Committee on the Rights of the Child, *Concluding Observations: Sweden*, (UN Doc No CRC/C/SWE/CO/4, 2009) paras 48 & 49.

[36] It is not the only example of Sweden ignoring human rights mechanisms' recommendations relating to drug policy. Following visits to Swedish prisons in 2003, for example, the Committee for the Prevention of Torture raised concerns about the lack of harm reduction services available such as opioid substitution therapy, CPT/Inf (2004, 32), para. 73 and that such treatment was discontinued upon incarceration (para. 137). In response to the CPT's request for more information the Government said that 'The National Board of Institutional Care, which has established that LVM (1988:870 *Care of Alcoholics, Drug Abusers and Abusers of Volatile Solvents Act*) is an enforcement law and which hardly applies with functioning substitution therapy, otherwise refrains from commenting concerning the existing regulations' CPT/Inf (2004) 33) 29. Opioid substitution therapy (with methadone, buprenorphine or other medications) is a proven opiate dependence treatment, and overdose and HIV prevention strategy. To date, OST in Swedish prisons remains rare and inadequate.

[37] M. Larsson, Speech at 54th session of the UN Commission on Narcotic Drugs, Vienna, 21 March 2011. http://www.sweden.gov.se/sb/d/14633/a/164448.

[38] CND is a functional commission of ECOSOC made up of fifty-three member states meeting once a year in Vienna. The CND is the governing body of the UN drug control programme, which is a major component of the work of the UN Office on Drugs and Crime.

[39] UN Commission on Narcotic Drugs, '*Youth and drugs: A global overview, Report of the Secretariat*' (UN Doc No E/CN.7/1999/8, 1999).

[40] UN General Assembly, 'Declaration on the Guiding Principles of Drug Demand Reduction', (UN Doc No A/RES/S-20/3, 1998), para. 13.

[41] Ibid. Annex, para. 3.

17. During the 53rd session of the CND in 2010, a resolution entitled 'Measures to protect children and young people from drug abuse' was debated.[42] It opened with a reference to article 33 but despite the broad nature of the title, and a reference to the use of children in trafficking in operative paragraph two, the text of the resolution was almost entirely about primary prevention with an even narrower focus on information campaigns (which, alone, are of limited value). To its credit, the UN Office on Drugs and Crime, in a report submitted to the 54th session of the CND based on this resolution, devoted considerable attention to treatment, rehabilitation and the prevention on HIV and other blood borne viruses.[43] The CRC, however, was not mentioned.

18. The International Narcotics Control Board (INCB, the independent treaty body for the three UN drug conventions) has also invoked article 33. At the 52nd session of the CND, Professor Hamid Ghodse, the INCB President at the time, provided the Board's opening address. While the INCB's formulation of article 33 was not a problem, the way in which it was used was questionable. The Board emphasised that human rights must be respected in drug control measures, and this is very much to be welcomed.[44] But its contention in this regard was that 'Controlling drugs and protecting human rights are not opposites but go hand in hand'.[45] This, however, is far from clear cut. There are areas of convergence, such as article 33 or the right to health (article 24 CRC; article 12 International Covenant on Economic Social and Cultural Rights), but whether drug control measures contribute to the realisation of these rights is always open and should inform policy decisions. There are

---

[42] CND Res 53/10 'Measures to protect children and young people from drug abuse', in Economic and Social Council, Official Records 2010, Supplement no. 8, 'Report of the 53rd Session of the Commission on Narcotic Drugs, (UN Doc No E/2010/28–E/CN.7/2010/18, 2010), 30–32.

[43] 'Measures to protect children and young people from drug abuse: Report of the Executive Director', UN Doc No. E/CN.7/2011/13, 2011).

[44] The INCB is not known for its reputation in this field. It has been criticised for its stances on human rights and HIV prevention, its secretive working methods and lack of transparency. There are currently no international lawyers on the Board. See D. Barrett, *Unique in International Relations? A comparison of the International Narcotics Control Board and the UN Human Rights Treaty Bodies*, (London, Harm Reduction International, 2007); J. Csete and D. Wolfe *Closed to reason: The International Narcotics Control Board and HIV/AIDS* (Toronto and New York, Canadian HIV/AIDS Legal Network and International Harm Reduction Development Program, 2007).

[45] Statement by Professor Hamid Ghodse, President International Narcotics Control Board (INCB) at the high-level segment of the 52nd session of the Commission on Narcotic Drugs on 11 March 2009, Vienna-Austria. The INCB is an independent quasi-judicial committee made up of thirteen members acting independently of governments. Formed under the 1961 Single Convention on Narcotic Drugs it has predecessors dating back to the League of Nations. www.incb.org.

also areas of unresolved conflict, including interferences with privacy,[46] religious freedom and indigenous and cultural rights[47] which require focused human rights scrutiny. The INCB's use of article 33 was to defend against any claims of a 'right to use drugs', a rather inaccurate, simplistic caricature of these concerns,[48] and an apparent assertion that article 33 blandly supports the status quo and justifies these restrictions on other fundamental rights.

19. Like the Commission on Narcotic Drugs, the INCB has also equated article 33 with efforts to prevent drug use—a somewhat trite position that fails to do justice to the full potential of the article.[49] On the other hand, in its thematic focus on primary prevention among children presented to Member States in 2010, the Board failed to mention the CRC at all.[50]

---

[46] For example, relating to possession of small amounts of drugs for personal use. Article 3(2) of the 1988 Convention Against the Illicit Traffic in Narcotic Drugs and Psychotropic Substances requires that possession be made a criminal offence, subject to constitutional principles—an important limitation clause. In Argentina criminalisation of such possession has been recently deemed unconstitutional. Arriola, Sebastián y otros s/ causa n° 9080, 25 de agosto de 2009, A. 891. XLIV.

[47] See further para. 184.

[48] Some have argued for an explicit human right to use drugs recreationally. John Holt, for example, argued for a right to use drugs for young people in his book *Escape from Childhood* (New York, Ballantine Book, 1974). Upon reading, however, what is being argued in most cases does not appear to be a *right* at all—but legal *permission* in limited, regulated contexts. See also, for example, R. Newcombe, *Details of 10 Specific Rights of Drug Users*, (Manchester, England, Lifeline, May 2007).

[49] See for example the Board's *Annual Report for 2008*, (UN Doc No E/INCB/2008/1, 2008), para. 35 'The issue of cannabis is closely related to the challenge of primary prevention for young people and other groups vulnerable to illicit drug use, given that cannabis tends to be the first and most widely used illicit drug. The welfare and protection of the young are priorities within the United Nations treaty system: the Convention on the Rights of the Child (art. 33) requires parties to the Convention to 'take all appropriate measures, including legislative, administrative, social and educational measures, to protect children from the illicit use of narcotic drugs and psychotropic substances . . . and to prevent the use of children in the illicit production and trafficking of such substances'.

[50] International Narcotics Control Board, *Annual Report for 2009*, (UN Doc No. E/INCB/2009/1, 2010), ch. 1.

CHAPTER TWO

COMPARISON WITH RELATED HUMAN RIGHTS PROVISIONS

1. *Relationship to Other International Instruments*

20. Central to this aspect of the discussion are of course the three UN drug conventions given their subject matter: the 1961 Single Convention on Narcotic Drugs; the 1971 Convention on Psychotropic Substances; and the 1988 Convention Against the Illicit Traffic in Narcotic Drugs and Psychotropic Substances. A closer look at their texts, however, shows how little of a focus there was on children during the drafting processes. Only one of the three drug conventions specifically refers to children—the 1988 trafficking convention, which contains two mentions.[51] Neither clause refers to measures to address drug use among children. One is a preambular statement. The other refers both to a specific prevention measure, and to the victimisation or use of minors in certain offences. In dealing with aspects of prevention and involvement in the drug trade, both relate to the protections afforded by article 33.

21. In its preamble the 1988 Convention states the drafters' deep concern about 'the fact that children are used in many parts of the world as an illicit drug consumers market and for purposes of illicit production, distribution and trade in narcotic drugs and psychotropic substances, which entails a danger of incalculable gravity'. It is a preambular statement, so not legally binding, but it provides context. The role of the child in providing moral justification for the provisions that follow is clear. It should be borne in mind that the 1988 treaty is arguably the most prescriptive and punitive of the three drug conventions.[52]

22. Article 3(5) of the same treaty, meanwhile, requires that 'The Parties shall ensure that their courts and other competent authorities having jurisdiction can take into account factual circumstances which make the

---

[51] There are no mentions in any of adolescent, young people, youth or other terms. 'Minor' also appears once in the 1988 convention and is quoted here.

[52] For an overview see N. Boister, *Penal Aspects of the UN Drug Conventions* (The Hague, London, Boston: Kluwer Law International, 2001).

commission of the offences established in accordance with paragraph 1[53] of this article particularly serious, such as:...(f) The victimization or use of minors; (g) The fact that the offence is committed in a penal institution or in an educational institution or social service facility or in their immediate vicinity or in other places to which school children and students resort for educational, sports and social activities'.

Sub-paragraph (f), refers to the involvement of minors in the production or trafficking in drugs, and is therefore closely related to the second clause of article 33 of the CRC. Article 3(c) of ILO Convention 182 (1999)[54] defines 'the use, procuring or offering of a child for illicit activities, in particular for the production and trafficking of drugs as defined in the relevant international treaties' as a worst form of child labour and therefore also supports this element of article 33. It is therefore more than clear from three separate treaties, and it must be said, basic child protection considerations, that the use of children in illicit production and trafficking in controlled substances is to be prevented. We return below to this discussion and what may be considered 'appropriate measures', in a child rights sense, to achieve this obligation.

Sub-paragraph (g) is related to prevention of drug use, aiming to deter sales to children. This, too, relates to the prevention element of article 33. Note, however, that the situation of children in fact using drugs is not referred to. The official commentary on the treaty sheds little further light.[55]

---

[53] Article 3(1) reads:

'Each Party shall adopt such measures as may be necessary to establish as criminal offences under its domestic law, when committed intentionally:

a) i) The production, manufacture, extraction; preparation, offering, offering for sale, distribution, sale, delivery on any terms whatsoever, brokerage, dispatch, dispatch in transit, transport, importation or exportation of any narcotic drug or any psychotropic substance contrary to the provisions of the 1961 Convention, the 1961 Convention as amended or the 1971 Convention;

ii) The cultivation of opium poppy, coca bush or cannabis plant for the purpose of the production of narcotic drugs contrary to the provisions of the 1961 Convention and the 1961 Convention as amended;

iii) The possession or purchase of any narcotic drug or psychotropic substance for the purpose of any of the activities enumerated in i) above;

iv) The manufacture, transport or distribution of equipment, materials or of substances listed in Table I and Table II, knowing that they are to be used in or for the illicit cultivation, production or manufacture of narcotic drugs or psychotropic substances;

v) The organization, management or financing of any of the offences enumerated in i), ii), iii) or iv) above'.

[54] Convention Concerning the Prohibition and Immediate Action for the Elimination of the Worst Forms of Child Labour (ILO No. 182), 2133 U.N.T.S.161, *entered into force* Nov. 19, 2000.

[55] United Nations, *Commentary on the United Nations Convention Against the Illicit Traffic in Narcotic Drugs and Psychotropic Substances 1988*, (New York, UN, 1998), pp. 15, 92, 93.

23. The fact that these are the only specific mentions of children in the drug treaties does not mean that their provisions do not apply to children. The specific situations of youth are raised in the political declaration on drugs, the guiding principles of demand reduction and the plan of action all adopted during the UN General Assembly Special Session (UNGASS) on Drugs in 1998,[56] and in the political declaration and plan of action adopted as the result of a high level review process in 2009.[57] All are based on the drug conventions as their legal framework. The question, however, is *how* the provisions of the drug conventions apply to children. This is an important dynamic between the two sets of international law and we return to this in more detail below.[58]

24. The WHO Framework Convention on Tobacco Control[59] specifically includes mention of the CRC in its preamble, recalling 'that the Convention on the Rights of the Child, adopted by the United Nations General Assembly on 20 November 1989, provides that States parties to that Convention recognize the right of the child to the enjoyment of the highest attainable standard of health'. It also contains lengthy provisions (article 16) relating to sales to and by children. In focusing on these dual aspects of use and involvement in trade, it too reflects the protections in article 33 relating to the illicit use, production and trafficking in narcotic drugs and psychotropic substances. A key question in relation to the FCTC, one with important implications, is whether it is a 'relevant international treaty' for the purposes of article 33. We return to this specific question below.[60]

25. By virtue of article 41 of the CRC, international treaties that provide greater protection for the rights of the child are brought into play. While the International Covenant on Economic Social and Cultural Rights (ICESCR) does not specifically refer to drugs, the Concluding Observations of the CESCR Committee do shed some light on the application of article 12 (the right to health) and article 15(1)(b) (the right to benefit from scientific progress and its applications) to the issue, as does General Comment No. 14

---

[56] All available at http://www.unodc.org/pdf/report_1999-01-01_1.pdf.

[57] 'Political Declaration and Plan of Action on International Cooperation towards an Integrated and Balanced Strategy to Counter the World Drug Problem', adopted at the High Level Segment of the UN Commission on Narcotic Drugs, 11–12 March 2009 available in the Report of the 52nd Session of the Commission on Narcotic Drugs, (UN Doc No E/2009/28—E/CN.7/2009/12, 2010).

[58] See 3.3.3 and 3.3.4.

[59] Adopted unanimously by the 56th World Health Assembly on 21 May 2003. The final text is contained in World Health Assembly Resolution 56.1.

[60] See paras 163–166.

on the right to health,[61] which is very instructive and helpful when read in the context of drug policies. Commenting on Mauritius in 2010 the CESCR Committee recommended that the State party, in order to progressively realise these rights, must 'Remove age barriers to accessing opioid substitution therapy and develop youth-friendly harm reduction services tailored to the specific needs of young people who use drugs'.[62] It would later be followed by similar recommendations by the Committee on the Rights of the Child relating to Ukraine.[63]

26. Like the ICESCR, the International Covenant on Civil and Political Rights (ICCPR) is applicable insofar as the rights contained in the treaty are engaged by drug policies. In 2010, for example, the Human Rights Committee raised concerns about the use of the military in fighting organised crime in Mexico.[64] Again, this was mirrored not long after by the Committee on the Rights of the Child, reviewing Mexico under the Optional Protocol to the CRC on the involvement of children in armed conflict. This, in turn, highlighted the relevance of the OPAC to the drug trade. The Committee criticised the use of children in fighting against the drug cartels.[65]

27. The Convention Against Torture may also apply where torture or cruel inhuman or degrading treatment or punishment are inflicted upon children—as 'drug dependence treatment', in the context of policing or otherwise (as would the ICCPR and regional human rights instruments). In 2010 the Committee Against Torture reviewed Cambodia's implementation of the Convention. It raised concerns about police round-ups of street children and people who use drugs, and the lack of inspection of drug rehabilitation centres.[66] Human Rights Watch had earlier in the year uncovered abuses of children in such centres.[67] In June 2011 the CRC Committee released its Concluding Observations following the submission of Cambodia's second periodic report. In its strongest statement yet on the abuse of children in the

---

[61] Committee on Economic Social and Cultural Rights, *General Comment No. 14: The right to the highest attainable standard of health*, (UN Doc No E/C.12/2000/4, 2000).

[62] Committee on Economic Social and Cultural Rights, *Concluding Observations: Mauritius* (UN Doc No E/C.12/MUS/CO/4, 2010), para. 27(c).

[63] Committee on the Rights of the Child, *Concluding Observations: Ukraine*, (UN Doc No CRC/C/UKR/CO/4, 2011), paras 59 & 60.

[64] Human Rights Committee, *Concluding Observations: Mexico* (UN Doc No CCPR/C/MEX/CO/5, 2010) para. 11.

[65] *Concluding Observations: Mexico* (OPAC) o.c. (note 18), para. 29.

[66] Committee Against Torture, *Concluding Observations: Cambodia* (UN Doc No CAT/C/KHM/CO/2, 2011), paras 11 & 20.

[67] *Skin on the Cable* o.c. (note 25).

name of drug treatment, the Committee raised its 'deep concern about allegations that children and adolescent addicted to drugs, children with mental disabilities and children in street situations have been subjected to torture and ill-treatment, including widespread beatings, whippings and administration of electric shock in drug rehabilitation and youth centres where some of them had been forcibly placed'. The Committee recommended that 'children in any form of arbitrary detention, whether in drug treatment and rehabilitation, social rehabilitation or any other type of Government-run centre are released without delay' and that Cambodia 'ensure prompt investigation into allegations of ill treatment and torture of children in those centers and that perpetrators are brought to justice.'[68]

28. Given that children who use drugs may be committing a crime through possession of drugs, or through acquisitive crime related to drug dependence, international juvenile justice standards of course must be brought into play. The same applies to children in fact involved in the drug trade (though article 33 refers to the *prevention* of the use of children in this way, rather than addressing explicitly this situation). If children who use drugs are deprived of their liberty (as a last resort and for the shortest time required) then their medical and health needs must be taken care of. Specific provisions relating to juveniles' health-related rights are contained in the 'Beijing Rules' (UN Standard Minimum Rules on the Administration of Juvenile Justice)[69] and the 'Havana Rules' (UN Rules for the Protection of Juveniles Deprived of their Liberty).[70] The Havana Rules specifically require drug dependence treatment for juveniles in places of detention. Rule 51 states that 'the medical services provided to juveniles should seek to detect and should treat any physical or mental illness, substance abuse or other condition.' Rule 54 further states that 'Juvenile detention facilities should adopt specialized drug abuse prevention and rehabilitation programmes administered by qualified personnel. These programmes should be adapted to the age, sex and other requirements of the juveniles concerned, and detoxification facilities and services staffed by trained personnel should be available to drug- or alcohol-dependent juveniles'. The newly adopted UN Rules for the Treatment of Women Prisoners and Non-Custodial Measures for Women Offenders (the

---

[68] Committee on the Rights of the Child, *Concluding Observations: Cambodia* (UN Doc No CRC/C/KHM/CO/2, 2011) paras 55 & 56.

[69] UN General Assembly, 'United Nations standard minimum rules for the administration of juvenile Justice' (UN Doc No GA/RES/40/33, 1985).

[70] UN General Assembly 'United Nation rules for the protection of juveniles deprived of their liberty' (UN Doc No GA/RES/45/113, 1990).

Bangkok Rules)[71] also apply. The rules contain specific provisions relating to drugs (e.g. Rule 6d on medical screening).

29. Regional human rights treaties also contain specific references to drugs. Article 28 of the African Charter on the Rights and Welfare of the Child, for example, closely reflects article 33 of the CRC: 'States parties to the present Charter shall take all appropriate measures to protect the child from the use of narcotics and illicit use of psychotropic substances as defined in the relevant international treaties, and to prevent the use of children in the production and trafficking of such substances.'[72] There are, however, noticeable differences. For example, the word 'illicit' is only used for psychotropic substances indicating some existing forms of licit use, while this is not allowed for narcotics. This may not have been intended. Surely children are not supposed to be protected from medical (licit) uses of narcotics such as morphine? The word illicit is also missing from production and trafficking. But again, was licit production intended to be captured by article 28? The article requires its own commentary.

30. Article 39(f) of the Arab Charter on Human Rights (2004), meanwhile, places the 'Fight against tobacco, drugs, and psychotropic substances' within the right to health. It does not specifically refer to children and drugs. The treaty unfortunately allows for the juvenile death penalty (article 7), contradicting article 37(a) of the CRC.[73]

31. Article 5 of the European Convention on Human Rights also warrants mention. In the context of the right to liberty and security of the person it provides (sub-paragraph e) for 'the lawful detention of persons for the prevention of the spreading of infectious diseases, of persons of unsound mind, alcoholics or drug addicts or vagrants'.[74] This, however, is not without qualification and important standards have been developed since the Convention was adopted in 1950.[75] This is crucial in the present context given the

---

[71] Economic and Social Council (ECOSOC), Resolution 2010/16, (UN Doc No E/RES/2010/16, 2010), *Annex.*

[72] African Charter on the Rights and Welfare of the Child, OAU Doc. CAB/LEG/24.9/49 (1990), *entered into force* Nov. 29, 1999.

[73] League of Arab States, Arab Charter on Human Rights, May 22, 2004, *reprinted in* 12 Int'l Hum. Rts. Rep. 893 (2005), *entered into force* March 15, 2008.

[74] Convention for the Protection of Human Rights and Fundamental Freedoms, 213 U.N.T.S. 222, *entered into force* Sept. 3, 1953, *as amended by* Protocols Nos 3, 5, 8, and 11 *which entered into force* on 21 September 1970, 20 December 1971, 1 January 1990, and 1 November 1998 *respectively.*

[75] See for example, UN Principles for the Protection of Persons with Mental Illness and for the Improvement of Mental Health Care, (UN Doc No A/RES/46/119, 1991) *Annex.*

widespread use of administrative detention against people who use drugs and street children.

32. The European Court of Human Rights has made a number of decisions in the context of drug policies relating, for example, to medical assistance to treat withdrawal,[76] and abusive measures to extract drugs that had been swallowed by a suspect.[77]

33. 'Illicit drug trafficking' is included in the Treaty of Lisbon (Article 69 B) as a 'particularly serious crime with a cross border dimension' over which the European Parliament and Council may 'establish minimum rules concerning the definition of criminal offences and sanctions'.[78] This commitment expands upon previous references to co-operation in the field of drug control in the Treaties of Maastricht[79] and Amsterdam.[80]

2. Relationship to Other Articles of the CRC

34. A wide range of articles in the CRC are connected to article 33 and are vital for interpreting the provision correctly. It is an analysis that shows just how cross-cutting an issue drug policy is, and, indeed, how useful a framework the CRC may be for policy guidance. We consider some of the connections briefly here and return to these articles and others throughout the commentary.

Article 3 (Best Interests of the Child)

35. Geraldine van Bueren writes that article 3 (1) 'does not create rights or duties, it is only a principle of interpretation which has to be considered in all actions concerning children'.[81] Drugs and drug policies certainly concern children—from drug use among them, to use within families and the community, to drug related crime and the drug trade. It is not in a child's best

---

[76] McGlinchey v UK (2003) 37 EHRR 41.

[77] Jalloh v. Germany, application no. 54810/00, 11 July 2006.

[78] Treaty of Lisbon Amending the Treaty on European Union and the Treaty Establishing the European Community, 13 December 2007, 2007/C 306/01.

[79] Articles 129, K.1(4 & 9)(Title VI).

[80] Article 152 (ex Article 129) which introduced a harm reduction perspective. The article referred to European Community action to complement 'action in reducing drugs-related health damage' (art 152.1) which was a significant move from the Maastricht reference to 'drug dependence' as one of the 'major health scourges' (art 129.1). The Lisbon treaty did not amend this aspect of the Treaty of Amsterdam.

[81] G. Van Bueren, The International Law on the Rights of the Child, (Dordrecht, London, Martinus Nijhoff and Save the Children, 1995).

interests to use drugs or to be involved in the illicit drug trade. Let us take that as self-evident and, indeed, the basis for article 33.

36. But it is not sufficient to stop there. As with so many areas the best interests principle raises many important questions: How does the best interests principle direct interpretation of international agreements on drugs? How does the principle shape drug laws and policies at national level? How does it shape programmatic responses to drug use among children and involvement in the drug trade? What about measures to tackle the drug trade more broadly? Does the best interests of the child come into play when sentencing primary care-givers for drug offences? How are the best interests of the child served in the context of parental drug dependence? Are there conflicts between the best interests of certain groups of children or individuals?

We explore many of these questions throughout this commentary.

Article 2 (*Non-Discrimination*)

37. Drug use and involvement in criminality carry considerable stigma—both for children using drugs or children who have committed crimes, and also those whose parents may use drugs, or may be incarcerated. Children should not be discriminated against on these bases. They should also not be discriminated against based on age. Many countries, however, have failed to implement specialised youth-focused drug dependence treatment and harm reduction services to address drug dependence among children and young people, and the potential harms associated with recreational drug use.

38. Article 2 also requires appropriately disaggregated data on drug use and involvement in the drug trade in order to identify patterns of vulnerability and target responses.[82] This, however, is rarely available in the context of drug use or drug related harms. There are many reasons for this, including the difficulty of collecting data on criminalised activity[83]—this is particularly so in relation to child involvement in the drug trade[84]—the stigma attached

---

[82] Committee on the Rights of the Child, General Comment No. 5 *General Measures of Implementation of the Convention on the Rights of the Child* (UN Doc No CRC/GC/2003/5, 2003).

[83] See for example the recent Swedish study on drug use in the country which failed to reach 'hidden drug users'. 'Narcotics Use in Sweden', Swedish National Institute of Public Health, December 2010. The study referred to problematic drug use as contributing to 'extensive social exclusion' (at p. 17 of the English summary).

[84] In relation to women and girls, see for example, UN Office on Drugs and Crime 'Promoting international cooperation in addressing the involvement of women and girls in drug trafficking, especially as couriers: Note of the Executive Director' (UN Doc No E/CN.7/2011/7, 2011), para. 11 'It will be possible to draw a more comprehensive picture at the global level only when countries improve their reporting systems. To that end, countries should be encour-

to drug use, and problems with data collection methodology. Criminal laws relating to drug use or certain services can impede such data collection. For example, legal age restrictions on harm reduction services (de facto discriminatory in themselves) can result in service providers not asking clients their age in order to provide them with assistance.

Article 6 (*the Right to Life, Survival and Development*)

39. The right to development dates back to the 'Declaration of Geneva' of 1924 (drafted by Eglantyne Jebb, the founder of the Save the Children movement): 'the child shall enjoy special protection and shall be given opportunities...to develop...in a healthy and normal manner and in conditions of freedom and dignity'. Within this context addressing drug use among children and young people is a priority. But as we explore below, it is important to distinguish between drug dependence and recreational drug use. The latter is becoming an ever more normal aspect of life for many adolescents and young adults. If this is the case then to ignore it is to miss an opportunity to intervene in a manner that makes sense to the young person, and that relates to their patterns of use. Problematic drug use and drug dependence among children and young people, on the other hand, requires specialised services which are absent in country after country worldwide.

40. Alfhild Petrén and Roger Hart are of the opinion that the CRC presents development as a continuing process of interaction between the individual child (with her or his inherent characteristics) and the immediate and larger environment.[85] As such, drug dependence within the family and community as well as drug related crime and violence will have an impact on the development of the child. But it is important to note that drug laws and policies, even if intended to protect children, can and do also have negative impacts on the child's environment and their development. Policing, sentencing and provision of healthcare among many other areas of policy, all impact on the child's survival and development.

---

aged to expand the information they regularly collect on drug traffickers to include gender and age and other aspects that can better describe the role, social circumstances and social status of women and men in criminal organizations.'

[85] Alfhild Petrén and Roger Hart, 'The Child's Right to development', in Alfhild Petrén and James Himes (eds) *Children's Rights: Turning Principles into Practice*, (Stockholm and Katmandu, Save the Children Sweden and UNICEF Regional Office for South Asia, 2000).

Article 12 (*Respect for the Views of the Child*)

41. A recent General Assembly resolution urged the Member States 'to strengthen or establish, in collaboration with young people and youth-led organisations, youth friendly substance abuse prevention programmes and affordable treatment and rehabilitation programmes'.[86] But children and young people are rarely, if ever, listened to in drug policy formation.[87] (Some youth-led organisations, however, have developed their own drug policy strategies and are actively involved in international advocacy.)[88] It is a considerable omission as children and young people will have valuable insights into drug use, involvement in the drug trade as well as experiences of law enforcement. A recent study undertaken by the European Monitoring Centre for Drugs and Drug Addiction (an institute of the European Union) which documented children's voices in relation to drug use, exemplified 'the value of taking into account the many varied perspectives and circumstances of children when planning effective interventions for them'.[89]

42. But article 12 applies not just to policy in this context but also to interventions to address drug use or dependence among individuals. The CRC Committee was clear in General Comment No. 12 that the right to be heard applies to healthcare settings and 'applies to individual health-care decisions, as well as to children's involvement in the development of health policy and services'.[90] The Committee went on to say that 'Children, including young children, should be included in decision-making processes, in a manner consistent with their evolving capacities. They should be provided with information about proposed treatments and their effects and outcomes'.[91] Confidential services, without parental consent, should be available to allow young people to listen and speak freely about the options available to them,

---

[86] UN General Assembly resolution 64/130, *Policies and programmes involving youth*, (UN Doc No A/RES/64/130, 2010).

[87] V. Staelens, 'Participation and protection of children against substance abuse and trafficking and production by children', in: F. Ang, et al., *Participation Rights of Children*, (Antwerp and Oxford, Intersentia, 2006) 109–122.

[88] For example, Youth RISE, a youth-led international network focusing on harm reduction and drug policies www.youthrise.org. See also Espolea, *Youth recommendations for an addiction prevention policy* (Mexico City, August 2010).

[89] European Monitoring Centre for Drugs and Drug Addiction, *Children's Voices, Experiences and Perceptions of European Children on Drugs and Alcohol Issues*, (Lisbon/Luxembourg, EMCDDA/ The Publications Office of the European Union, 2010).

[90] Committee on the Rights of the Child, *General Comment No. 12: the right of the child to be heard*, (UN Doc No CRC/C/GC/12, 2009), para. 98.

[91] Ibid. para. 100.

and about ways to protect themselves.[92] It should be borne in mind also that peer-based education is an important intervention, requiring the full acceptance of youth participation. Similarly, and in line with the evolving capacities of the child, clinical decisions about a child's treatment should be made as far as possible taking into account the views of the child. Neither age nor drug dependence of themselves are sufficient reasons to ignore this obligation. The presumption must be in favour of the child having capacity to consent to medical treatment and clear guidelines should be established for ascertaining such capacity.[93]

Article 5 (*Evolving Capacities of the Child*)

43. Children require varying degrees of protection, participation and opportunity for autonomy in different contexts and across different areas of decision-making.[94] Some adolescents are more at risk than others. Those with early maturation are more likely to be engaged in substance use (more than peers who mature somewhat later), for example.[95] Young children are at acute risk and it is clear that earlier use of drugs is a risk factor for later problems. It has been shown for example that both dosage of cannabis and the age of the first use were associated with psychotic experiences.[96]

45. As noted above, the evolving capacities of the child must also come into play in decisions on treatment and consultations with the child in question. But what about involvement in drug related crime? Here, the evolving capacities principle is intertwined with the minimum age of criminal responsibility and efforts to divert young people from the criminal justice system.

Article 17 (*the Right to Appropriate Information*)

46. Article 17 recognises the importance of mass media and requires protection from information or material injurious health and wellbeing. In the

---

[92] Ibid. para. 101.

[93] Ibid. para. 102. See also (from the UK) Gillick v West Norfolk and Wisbech Area Health Authority [1985] 3 All ER 402 (HL).

[94] G. Lansdown, *Understanding the concept of evolving capacities*, (New York/Florence, UNICEF, 2005).

[95] M. R. Hayatbakksh, et al., 'Early puberal maturation in the prediction of early adult substance use: a prospective study', *Addiction* (2009 (104) 59–66. See also: R. C. M. E. Engels, 'Commentary: Early Puberal Maturation and Drug use: Underlying Mechanisms', *Addiction* (2009 (104) 67–68.

[96] C. D. Schubart, W. A., et al., 'Cannabis use at a young age is associated with psychotic experiences', *Psychological Medicine*, (7 October 2010).

context of drugs and children the most common concern is 'glamorisation' of drug use or, indeed, of involvement in the drug trade. In relation to drug use this is highly exaggerated when compared with alcohol, and it is difficult to know what role the media and movies have on children's views of the drug trade. But it is important to consider also the increasing role of digital media in a time when children are 'multitasking'.

47. There is a need for responsible media reporting about drugs and drug use. Too often this is sensationalised and inaccurate. It can also be abusive.[97] According to the CRC Committee, information on drugs should be 'accurate and objective'.[98] This is not just about prevention, but also young people currently using drugs, or currently in possession of them. The right information about a certain drug or psychotropic substance can prevent a lot of harm. The CRC Committee recently recommended that Finland work with mass media to 'ensure their contribution to healthy lifestyles and consumption patterns by children and adolescents'.[99]

Article 18(2) (*Assistance to Parents/Guardians in Child-Rearing*)

48. The harms to children associated with parental drug dependence are clear. As we argue below, protecting children from the illicit use of narcotic drugs must also include protection in the context of drug use within the family. An important question that arises is what may be required to 'render appropriate assistance to parents and legal guardians in the performance of their child-rearing responsibilities' in the context of drug (or alcohol) dependence.

---

[97] A recent example from Ireland illustrates the point. The Irish Independent newspaper published an article in which the author said 'I hate junkies more than anything else', called them 'worthless' 'vermin', said he would cheer if they were all to die, and called for them to be sterilised. Ian O'Doherty 'Sterilising junkies may seem harsh, but it does make sense' *Irish Independent*, 18 February 2011.

[98] This is a consistent feature in the Committee's Concluding Observations. See for example, over the last decade: *Slovakia* (UN Doc No CRC/C/15/ADD.140, 2000) para. 42; *Estonia* (UN Doc No CRC/C/15/ADD.196, 2003) para. 50; *Pakistan* (UN Doc No CRC/C/15/ADD.217, 2003) para. 73; *Indonesia* (UN Doc No CRC/C/15/ADD.223, 2004) para. 74; *Norway* (UN Doc No CRC/C/15/Add.263, 2005) para. 44; *Denmark* (UN Doc No CRC/C/DNK/CO/3, 2005) para. 55; *Belize* (UN Doc No CRC/C/15/Add.252, 2005) para. 55; *Russian Federation* (UN Doc No CRC/C/RUS/CO/3, 2005) para. 77; *Kiribati* (UN Doc No CRC/C/KIR/CO/1, 2006) para. 49; *Sweden* (UN Doc No CRC/C/SWE/CO/4, 2009) para. 49; *Tunisia* (UN Doc No CRC/C/TUN/CO/3, 2010) para. 54.

[99] UN Committee on the Rights of the Child, *Concluding Observations: Finland*, (UN Doc No CRC/C/FIN/CO/4, 2011) para. 49.

Article 19 (*Protection from Neglect and Violence*)

49. On a similar note, children of parents suffering from drug or alcohol dependence problems can and do experience neglect and violence as a result.[100] Children who use drugs also experience violence and neglect in many forms, in particular those most at risk, including children who live on the streets.[101] Involvement in the drug trade may also expose children to violence both from criminal gangs and from law enforcement. States must take appropriate measures to protect such children.

Art. 24 (*the Right to Health and Health Services*)

50. The connection between articles 24 and 33 has been specifically drawn by the CRC Committee in General Comment No. 3 on HIV/AIDS, and in the fact that the Committee now requests information on this aspect of article 33 under the basic health and welfare cluster for the purposes of periodic reporting.[102] The Committee on Economic Social and Cultural Rights has also addressed drug use under article 12 of the Covenant on Economic Social and Cultural Rights,[103] and both the present and former Special Rapporteurs on the Right to Health have addressed drug use as part of their mandate.[104] The relevance of the right to health in the context of drug use and dependence is clear. But what it requires of itself and what it means for the interpretation of article 33 requires development. What are available, accessible, acceptable and high quality services for children and parents who use drugs?

---

[100] See for example (from the UK), Childline Casenotes 'Children talking to ChildLine about parental alcohol and drug misuse' ChildI ine and NSPCC, August 2010; 'Hidden Harm: Responding to the needs of children of problem drug users' Report of an Inquiry by the Advisory Council on the Misuse of Drugs, 2003.

[101] See for example, UNICEF, *Blame and Banishment: The underground HIV epidemic facing children in Eastern Europe and Central Asia*, New York, 2010.

[102] Committee on the Rights of the Child, *CRC Treaty specific reporting guidelines, harmonised according to the common core document*, (UN Doc No CRC/C/58/Rev.2, 2010), para. 34(f).

[103] Committee on Economic Social and Cultural Rights, *Concluding Observations: Tajikistan* (UN Doc No E/C.12/TJK/CO/1, 2006) para. 70; *Ukraine* (UN Doc No E/C.12/UKR/CO/5, 2007) para. 28; *Poland* (UN Doc No E/C.12/POL/CO/5, 2009) para. 26; *Kazakhstan* (UN Doc No E/C.12/KAZ/CO/1, 2010) para. 34; *Mauritius* (UN Doc No E/C.12/MUS/CO/4, 2010) para. 27. See also *List of Issues on the fifth periodic report of the Russian Federation* (UN Doc No E/C.12/RUS/Q/5, 2010) para. 36.

[104] For example, Special Rapporteur on the right of everyone to the highest attainable standard of physical and mental health, Paul Hunt, Mission to Sweden (UN Doc No A/HRC/4/28/Add.2, 2007) paras 60–62; Special Rapporteur on the right of everyone to the highest attainable standard of physical and mental health, Anand Grover, Mission to Poland (UN Doc No A/HRC/14/20/Add.3, 2009) paras 57–80; and the Special Rapporteur's Annual Thematic Report to the UN General Assembly, (UN Doc No A/65/255, 2010), focusing on drug control.

Articles 26 (*Right to Social Security*) and 27 (*Right to an Adequate Standard of Living*)

51. Poverty and economic necessity are considerable drivers towards involvement in the drug trade, either at street level among street-involved children, in relation to transport in the form of drug 'mules'/carriers, or in rural settings in the production of subsistence crops such as coca and opium poppy. The response to this, however, is often rooted in law enforcement, reacting to the alleged crimes. A rights-based response demands focusing on root causes. Unfortunately, involvement in the drug trade can result in further rights violations and worsen the cycle of poverty. In Afghanistan, opium bans, forced eradication and threats of NATO bombing contributed to human displacement both internally and into neighbouring Pakistan.[105] There are now over four million internally displaced people in Colombia,[106] most due to drug fuelled civil conflict, many as a direct result of anti-narcotic efforts and aerial fumigation campaigns targeting coca.

Article 28 (*Right to Education*)

52. Absence from and, particularly, exclusion from education are risk factors for initiation into drug use. As such, school retention has an important protective role to play (one mirrored in HIV prevention). On the contrary, random drug testing in schools and searches of schoolbags and clothes are of doubtful benefit and can create distrust among those at risk, increasing absences. We discuss prevention education, random school drug testing, searches, and the protective role of education in more detail below.

Article 32 (*Freedom from Economic Exploitation*)

53. The second clause of article 33 requires protection from the use of children in the drug trade. Such involvement is therefore framed as a form of exploitation and is therefore closely connected with article 32. In turn, these provisions may be read alongside article 3 of ILO Convention 182 on the worst forms of child labour and article 3 of the 1988 Convention Against the Illicit Traffic in Narcotic Drugs and Psychotropic Substances—both of which include obligations to address such exploitation.

---

[105] V. Felbab-Brown 'U.S. Counternarcotics Strategy in Afghanistan', Testimony before the U.S. Senate Caucus on International Narcotics Control, 21 October 2009.

[106] UN Office for the Co-ordination of Humanitarian Affairs, *Colombia humanitarian situation, synopsis: January-June*, 2009.

Articles 37 (*freedom from torture of cruel inhuman or degrading treatment or punishment; freedom from arbitrary arrest or detention; rights of children deprived of their liberty*) and 40 (*juvenile justice*)

54. Involvement in the drug trade, and indeed, drug use, brings many children and young people into contact with criminality and the criminal justice system. Many suffer violence and abuse at the hands of gangs and other young people, but also law enforcement and personnel in detention facilities. All such abuse must, of course, be investigated, and those responsible held to account.

55. For children and young people who do come into contact with the criminal justice system, juvenile justice standards must be applied, including detention as a measure of last resort, and the right to a fair trial in a child-friendly justice system—often denied in the context of detention for drug dependence 'treatment' or 'sweeps' of street children.

Article 39 (*Physical and Psychological Recovery and Social Reintegration*)

56. For children who have been exploited in the drug trade, who have been living and/or working on the streets, or who have experienced violence or neglect in the home or in places of detention, there is an obligation on States parties to ensure their physical and psychological recovery and reintegration. It is an article that is closely connected with many others, but article 2 requires specific focus, given the intense stigma and discrimination associated with children who have been involved in criminality, street involved, drug dependent, or from homes within which drug dependence was a problem. In addition, social and community support for young people overcoming drug dependence problems is important if relapse and the risk of overdose is to be avoided, and if treatment programmes are to be adhered to.

CHAPTER THREE

SCOPE OF ARTICLE 33

1. *How the CRC Committee Has Dealt with Article 33*

57. In its first years of work article 33 was all but ignored by the Committee on the Rights of the Child. But in its 1996 guidelines to States parties on the form and contents of periodic reports, the Committee set out the information required in the context of article 33. This included a simple restatement of the provision but also went into more detail requesting information on relevant international and bilateral treaties; prevention and education; assistance to children and families; monitoring systems; and disaggregated data. Interestingly, the Committee also requested information on alcohol and tobacco.[107]

58. Since 1991, article 33 had been considered under the 'special protection measures' cluster of rights in the CRC in which the implementation of article 22 and articles 30–40 are to be reviewed. In October 2010, however, this changed. The Committee's harmonised 'Treaty-specific guidelines regarding the form and content of periodic reports to be submitted by States parties under article 44, paragraph 1 (b), of the Convention on the Rights of the Child' now splits article 33 in two.[108] The protection of children from the illicit use of drugs is dealt with under 'disability, basic health and welfare', while prevention of the use of children in illicit production and trafficking remains a 'special protection measure'. This is a positive move, more reflective of the reality of drug use among young people, and connecting more closely drug use and dependence to the social and health-related rights in the treaty.

59. The prevention of the use of children in the illicit production and trafficking in narcotic drugs and psychotropic substances remain a special

---

[107] Committee on the Rights of the Child, *General Guidelines Regarding the Form and Contents of Periodic Reports to be Submitted by States parties under article 44, paragraph 1 (b) of the Convention* (UN Doc No CRC/C/58, 1996).

[108] Committee on the Rights of the Child, *Treaty-specific guidelines regarding form and content of periodic reports to be submitted by States parties under article 44, paragraph 1 (b), of the Convention on the Rights of the Child* (CRC./C/58/Rev.2, 2010) paras 34(f) & 39(c)(ii).

protection measure. It is something the Committee has had less occasion to address (drug use among young people being a far more common and widespread phenomenon) and has rarely made any specific recommendations. It has on a number of occasions simply expressed concern without concrete recommendations.[109] In relation to the Russian Federation in 2005, for example, the Committee raised this concern but recommended that the State party 'take measures to prevent their involvement in drug trafficking'.[110] The Committee was more specific on Belarus in 2002, requesting that the State party 'Undertake a study on the issue of trafficking and trafficking-related problems, such as sexual exploitation, drug abuse and the involvement of children in the drug trade, and economic exploitation, in order to assess their scope and causes, and develop and implement effective monitoring and other measures to prevent them'.[111] As may be expected, more specific concerns have arisen in relation to Colombia and Mexico. In the case of the former the Committee expressed its alarm 'over the high number of children exposed to dangerous and/or degrading work such as agricultural labour in coca plantations' and its concern 'over the manufacture and the export of drugs from Colombia, which affects children who are pickers of coca leaves (*raspachines*), as well as children forced or lured into trafficking drugs, including within their bodies (*mulas*)'. The Committee's recommendations, however, were not as pointed, being general recommendations relating to economic exploitation.[112]

As noted above, the Committee has recently addressed drug trafficking in the context of the Optional Protocol on Children in Armed Conflict (OPAC) in Mexico. This was not, of course, based on article 33, but is directly related.[113]

60. In relation to drug use the Committee has now specifically requested that States parties take into account the General Comments on HIV/AIDS[114]

---

[109] For example, *Concluding Observations: Saint Lucia* (UN Doc No CRC/C/15/Add.258, 2005) para. 68; *Netherlands* (Netherlands Antilles) (UN Doc No CRC/C/15/ADD.186, 2002) paras 62 & 63.

[110] Committee on the Rights of the Child, *Concluding Observations: Russian Federation*, (UN Doc No CRC/C/RUS/CO/3, 2005) Para. 77.

[111] Committee on the Rights of the Child, *Concluding Observations: Belarus*, (UN Doc No CRC/C/15/Add.180, 2002) para. 51. See also *Concluding Observations: Guinea Bissau* (UN Doc No CRC/C/15/Add.177, 2002) paras 54 & 55.

[112] Committee on the Rights of the Child, *Concluding Observations: Colombia* (UN Doc No CRC/C/COL/CO/3, 2006) paras 82, 83, 88, 89.

[113] *Concluding Observations: Mexico* (OPAC), o.c. (note 18) para. 29.

[114] Committee on the Rights of the Child, *General Comment No. 3: HIV/AIDS and the Rights of the Child*, (UN Doc No CRC/GC/2003/3, 2003).

and adolescent health[115] (both from 2003) when reporting on the disability, basic health and welfare cluster. Both of these General Comments included drug use. In the context of HIV/AIDS, for example, this would indicate that the Committee now requires information on services focusing on HIV prevention among young people who inject drugs. As noted in General Comment No. 3 on HIV/AIDS 'Injecting practices using unsterilized instruments further increase the risk of HIV transmission. The Committee notes that greater understanding of substance use behaviours among children is needed, including the impact that neglect and violation of the rights of the child has on these behaviours. In most countries, children have not benefited from pragmatic HIV prevention programmes related to substance use, which even when they do exist have largely targeted adults.'[116]

61. The Committee went on to provide some normative guidance in the same paragraph, stating that 'policies and programmes aimed at reducing substance use and HIV transmission must recognize the particular sensitivities and lifestyles of children, including adolescents, in the context of HIV/AIDS prevention. Consistent with the rights of children under articles 33 and 24 of the Convention, States parties are obligated to ensure the implementation of programmes which aim to reduce the factors that expose children to the use of substances, as well as those that provide treatment and support to children who are abusing substances.'[117]

62. This comment remains one of the most detailed and helpful from the Committee on drug use. Its most explicit Concluding Observations on this aspect have been those adopted in February 2011 on Ukraine—some of the most detailed yet on problematic drug use from the Committee and worth setting out in full:

> The Committee is deeply concerned at the increasing practice of drug injection among children, affecting in particular children in prison, children left behind by migrating parents, children in street situations, and that drug use constitutes a main reason for HIV infection. It is deeply concerned at the lack of specialized youth-friendly services aimed at treatment and rehabilitation for these at-risk children, and that legal and attitudinal barriers impede access to such services (such as order of the Drug Enforcement Department of the Ministry of Internal Affairs no. 40/2/1-106 of 18 January 2011). The Committee

---

[115] Committee on the Rights of the Child, *General Comment No. 4: Adolescent health and development in the context of the Convention on the Rights of the Child*, (UN Doc No CRC/GC/2003/4, 2003).

[116] General Comment No. 3 o.c. (note 114) para. 39.

[117] Ibid.

is also concerned that the State party's drug strategy 2010–2015 fails to take these issues sufficiently into account and that new regulations relating to personal possession of drugs may bring more at risk adolescents into contact with the criminal justice system. In addition, the Committee is deeply concerned at the very high proportion of and early initiation age of tobacco and alcohol use among children, related in part to the ineffectiveness and weak enforcement of existing legislation prohibiting the sale of cigarettes and alcohol to children.

The Committee recommends that the State party, in partnership with non-governmental organizations, develop a comprehensive strategy for addressing the alarming situation of drug abuse among children and youth and undertake a broad range of evidence-based measures in line with the Convention, and to:

a. Develop specialised and youth-friendly drug dependence treatment and harm reduction services for children and young people, building on recent legislative progress on HIV/AIDS and the successful pilot programmes for most at risk adolescents initiated by UNICEF;
b. Ensure that criminal laws do not impede access to such services, including by amending laws that criminalise children for possession or use of drugs;
c. Ensure that health and law enforcement personnel working with at-risk children are appropriately trained in HIV prevention and that abuses by law enforcement against at risk children are investigated and punished;
d. Intensify enforcement of the prohibition of the sale of alcohol and tobacco to children and to address root causes to substance use and abuse among children and youth.'[118]

63. There have been other Concluding Observations from the Committee that, while more generally framed, assist in the development of normative guidance, including on recreational drug use, which is not a focus in the above recommendations, but forms the majority of drug use among young people. Many of these come through again and again. 'Accurate and objective information'[119] is a consistent feature, as is the recommendation that children who use drugs should be 'treated as victims and not as criminals'.[120] The Committee often calls for the diversion of such children from the criminal justice system. These might seem general, but they in fact challenge commonly used scare tactics and disproportionate law enforcement approaches.

---

[118] *Concluding Observations: Ukraine*, o.c. (note 63), paras 59 & 60.
[119] O.c. (note 98).
[120] For example: Committee on the Rights of the Child: *Concluding Observations: Armenia* (UN Doc No CRC/C/15/ADD.225, 2004) para. 63; *Indonesia* (UN Doc No CRC/C/15/ADD.223, 2004) para. 74; *Norway* (UN Doc No CRC/C/15/Add.263, 2005) para. 44; *Denmark* (UN Doc No CRC/C/DNK/CO/3, 2005) para. 55; *Russian Federation* (UN Doc No CRC/C/RUS/CO/3, 2005) para. 77; *Maldives* (UN Doc No CRC/C/MDV/CO/3, 2007) para. 88; *Marshall Islands* (UN Doc No CRC/C/MHL/CO/2, 2007) para. 55; *Afghanistan* (UN Doc No CRC/C/AFG/CO/1, 2011) para. 52(d).

The Concluding Observation on Ukraine above is the most explicit statement on this to date, however, calling directly for legislative change to decriminalise children who use drugs. The Committee is also consistent in its calls for treatment and rehabilitation for children who are drug dependent,[121] important given the frequent lack of specialised services for young people who use drugs.

64. General Comment no. 10 on juvenile justice from 2007, meanwhile, is explicitly connected to children deprived of their liberty for drug dependence treatment.[122] The General Comment on adolescent health is connected to this, referring to hospitalization or placement in a psychiatric institution.[123] According to the Committee 'this decision should be made in accordance with the principle of the best interests of the child'.

65. General Comment no. 4 on adolescent health from 2003 is not nearly as detailed on drug use as General Comment No. 3 but does recommend the prohibition of marketing of alcohol and tobacco to young people.[124] The Committee is consistent on this point, evidenced in the Concluding Observation on Ukraine above. It is one reflected also in the Framework Convention on Tobacco Control.

66. General Comment no. 7 on implementing child rights in early childhood refers to parental drug and alcohol dependence in the context of article 33.[125] It is an issue the Committee has recently taken up with the government of New Zealand, recommending that the State party 'intensify its efforts to render appropriate assistance to parents and legal guardians in the performance of their child-rearing responsibilities with timely responses at the local level, including...services for the treatment of alcohol- or drug-related

---

[121] For example: Committee on the Rights of the Child, *Concluding Observations: South Africa* (UN Doc No CRC/C/15/ADD.122, 2000) para. 38; *France* (UN Doc No CRC/C/15/ADD.240, 2004) para. 57; *Germany* (UN Doc No CRC/C/15/ADD.226, 2004) para. 43; *Thailand* (UN Doc No CRC/C/THA/CO/2, 2006) para. 54; *Peru* (UN Doc No CRC/C/PER/CO/3, 2006) para. 55; *Malaysia* (UN Doc No CRC/C/MYS/CO/1, 2007) para. 98; *Bangladesh* (UN Doc No CRC/C/BGD/CO/4, 2009) para. 66; *Cameroon* (UN Doc No CRC/C/CMR/CO/2, 2010) para. 57; *Tajikistan* (UN Doc No CRC/C/TJK/CO/2, 2010) para. 54; *Bahrain* (UN Doc No CRC/C/BHR/CO/2-3, 2011) paras 59 & 60.

[122] Committee on the Rights of the Child, *General Comment No. 10: Children's rights in juvenile justice* (UN Doc No CRC/C/GC/10, 2007).

[123] O.c. (note 115) para. 29.

[124] Ibid., para. 25.

[125] Committee on the Rights of the Child, *General Comment No. 7: Implementing child rights in early childhood* (UN Doc No CRC/C/GC7, 2005).

problems...'[126] In 2009, the Committee raised its concern about 'the large number of children who suffer as a result of their parents' drug abuse' in Sweden.[127] It recommended 'the provision of necessary evidence-based support, recovery and reintegration services to all children affected by substance abuse, including drug users below 18 years of age and children suffering as a result of their parents' drug abuse, aimed at effectively reducing the harmful consequences of such abuse.'[128]

67. Aside from notable exceptions including those set out here, the Committee's Concluding Observations on drug use have often been very general, sometimes no more than a restatement of article 33 itself,[129] a call to 'combat' drug abuse, or an expression of the Committee's concern about the high number of children who consume drugs in the State Party, followed by a recommendation of a general nature.[130] There has been a lack of focus on recreational drug use, with concerns and recommendations relating mainly to problematic drug use, injecting, and drug dependence. It must be recognised, however, that given the scope of the CRC and the volume of work before the Committee, it is reliant on quality information from States parties, UNICEF and other UN agencies, and from NGOs in the form of alternative reports, to facilitate detailed commentary. This has not been forthcoming consistently from these sources. On occasion a government will provide detailed information but this does not necessarily translate into

---

[126] Committee on the Rights of the Child, *Concluding Observations: New Zealand*, (UN Doc No CRC/C/NZL/CO/3-4, 2011) para. 31.

[127] Committee on the Rights of the Child, *Concluding Observations: Sweden* o.c. (note 35), para. 48.

[128] Ibid., para. 49.

[129] See for example the *Concluding Observations: Georgia* (UN Doc No CRC/C/15/ADD.124, 2000) para. 65, *Surinam* (UN Doc No CRC/C/15/ADD.130, 2000) para. 56; *South Africa* (UN Doc No CRC/C/15/ADD.122, 2000) para. 38; and *Grenada* (UN Doc No CRC/C/15/ADD.121, 2000) para. 27. All state 'In the light of article 33 of the Convention, the Committee recommends that the State party take all appropriate measures, including administrative, social and educational measures, to protect children from the illicit use of alcohol, narcotic drugs and psychotropic substances and to prevent the use of children in the illicit production and trafficking of such substances' adding general recommendations on rehabilitation and co-operation with international agencies.

[130] See for example, *Concluding Observations: Lao People's Democratic Republic* (UN Doc No CRC/C/LAO/CO/2, 2011) para. 60. A much used formulation or close variation thereof has been to 'take action to combat drug and alcohol abuse by children, including through public education awareness campaigns, and ensure that children who abuse alcohol and/or use drugs and other harmful substances have access to effective structures and procedures for treatment, counselling, recovery and reintegration'. See *Concluding Observations: Saint Vincent and the Grenadines* (UN Doc No CRC/C/15/ADD.184, 2002) para. 51; *Papua New Guinea* (UN Doc No CRC/C/15/ADD.229, 2004) para. 62; *Antigua and Barbuda* (UN Doc No CRC/C/15/ADD.247, 2004) para. 63; *Nigeria* (UN Doc No CRC/C/15/Add.257, 2005) para. 68.

detailed Concluding Observations from the Committee.[131] It is instructive that the Committee's detailed commentary on Ukraine in 2011 followed a specific alternative report submitted by a coalition of national and international NGOs working in the field[132] as did the Committee's concerns about Mexico's use of children in drug law enforcement.[133]

68. The general lack of information reaching the Committee may also contribute to the occasionally problematic recommendations that are made. In 2007 for example, in its Concluding Observations on Slovakia the Committee welcomed 'the fact that primary and secondary schools have coordinators for the prevention of *drug addiction and other sociopathic phenomena*' [emphasis added]. To refer to drug use or dependence as sociopathic is both incorrect and stigmatising and may have been corrected had information from NGOs working in the field been available. In 2002, in relation to the Philippines, the Committee recommended that the State party 'Combat drug and substance abuse among children and adolescents, for example *by effectively implementing the Comprehensive Dangerous Drugs Act of 2002*' [emphasis added]. The law in question included the death penalty for drug offences. It has since been abolished for all offences, but indicates a lack of awareness of the Committee of the context in which this recommendation was made.

69. The Committee's Concluding Observations (and the summary records of the meetings preceding these Concluding Observations), however, do reflect the development of the Committee's deliberations over the years. Mexico serves as an example. In the Concluding Observations in 1994 drug use was not mentioned.[134] In the Concluding Observations of 1999 on Mexico

---

[131] See for example, Government of Afghanistan, *Initial Report of the State Party: Afghanistan*, (Kabul/Geneva, 13 June, 2010) CRC/C/AFG/1. Paragraphs 327 and 329 on page 71. cf the Committee's Concluding Observations on Afghanistan adopted in 2011 in response to the government report (UN Doc No CRC/C/AFG/CO/1, 2011) paras 51(d) & 52(d).

[132] Eurasian Harm Reduction Network and Harm Reduction International, '*Briefing to the UN Committee on the Rights of the Child on Ukraine's 4th periodic report on the implementation of the Convention on the Rights of the Child: Injecting drug use, sex work and HIV among children and adolescents at risk*', (Vilnius/London, April 2010).

[133] V. Geremia, 'Children and Armed Conflict in Mexico: Alternative report on the implementation of the Optional Protocol to the Convention on the Rights of the Child on the involvement of children in armed conflict' Red Por Los Derechos De La Infancia en Mexico (REDIM), 2011.

[134] Committee on the Rights of the Child, *Concluding Observations: Mexico* (Geneva, UK, 7 February 1994) CRC/C/15/Add.13. The Second NGO Report to the CRC Committee in the situation of children in Mexico (from the Mexican Collective in Support of Children Comexani, january 2004) does discuss addictions: 'the trafficking and use of inhalables as a public health problem requires more strict action on the part of the government as well as the industries that produce the solvents. Society itself must become more involved in this area. The prob-

there was just one paragraph with praise to the government.[135] But in 2006 (although no mention was made of drug cartels/drug gang related violence) there was a long paragraph with six subsections. It included 'formulating a rights-based plan of action for the protection of children and adolescents from the dangers of drugs and harmful substances and involving children in its formulation and implementation'.[136] A similar trend can be seen by comparing the Ukraine Concluding Observations set out above with those of 2002; and those on Sweden from 2009[137] with the recommendations from 2005,[138] 1999,[139] and 1993.[140]

2. *Unpacking the Text*

70. To begin with it is important to note that the article contains *two* substantive protections:

1. Protection from the illicit use of narcotic drugs and psychotropic substances as defined in the relevant international treaties
2. Prevention of the use of children in the illicit production and trafficking of such substances.

We return to each of these in chapter three, but in the meantime a closer look at the text is required.

2.1. *'Shall Take All Appropriate Measures'*

71. It should be noted from the outset that the article is framed in strong terms. 'Shall' is the stronger formulation in the Convention, compared with

---

lem of the trafficking of inhalables deserves at least the same attention, budget and strong determination for action as the fight against the production and trafficking of drugs'.

[135] Committee on the Rights of the Child, *Concluding Observations: Mexico*, (Geneva, UN, 1999) CC/C/15/Add.112, para. 8.

[136] Committee on the Rights of the Child, *Concluding Observations: Mexico*, (Geneva, UN, 8 June 2006) CRC/C/MEX/CO/3, paragraph 67 (a–e).

[137] Concluding Observations: Sweden o.c. (note 35).

[138] Committee on the Rights of the Child, *Concluding Observations: Sweden* (UN Doc No CRC/C/15/Add.248, 2005) paras 33 & 34.

[139] Committee on the Rights of the Child, *Concluding Observations: Sweden* (UN Doc No CRC/C/15/Add.101, 1999) para. 21.

[140] Committee on the Rights of the Child, *Concluding Observations: Sweden* (UN Doc No CRC/C/15/Add.2, 1993) drug use not mentioned.

'undertake to ensure' in art 3(2), 'undertake to respect' in art 8(1) or 'recognize' in art 15(1).

72. The provision requires appropriate *action*. Omissions would fall foul of article 33. There are approximately two million injecting drug users in Russia, for example, many under eighteen, with around half living with HIV.[141] The Government refuses to take any measures to address this, spending nothing on needle and syringe programmes, and banning outright the use of opioid substitution therapy and even the promotion of such services until 2020.[142] Understanding omissions, however, demands scrutiny of positive obligations.

73. The phrase 'appropriate measures' frames article 33. It is an important qualifier, defending against arbitrariness, disproportionate measures and abuses of human rights in pursuit of protecting children from drugs or involvement in the drug trade. Importantly, it guides a child rights based approach to these issues. But the drafters never discussed the term in the context of this provision.

74. The CRC Committee has recently discussed the term briefly in its General Comment on article 19 (violence against children), stating that '[A]ppropriate *cannot* be interpreted to mean acceptance of some forms of violence' [emphasis in original].[143] Does the same finding apply to article 33? Certainly on the use of children in the drug trade (as a form of exploitation), but what about drug use among children and young people? While the wording is the same in each article (all appropriate measures ... to protect the child from ...), they relate to qualitatively different issues. One relates to violence inflicted upon children, the other to behaviours among them, and a category, for some, of vulnerability. The context is important. That drug use among children is not to be accepted is clear from the wording. But what does this mean in practice? What if a lack of acceptance translates into stigma and social marginalisation, as seen in relation to people who

---

[141] E. Holt, 'Russian injected drug use soars in face of political inertia', *The Lancet*, (3 July 2010 (376)) 9734, 13.

[142] See See for example, *Replies by the Government of the Russian Federation to the list of issues (E/C.12/RUS/Q/5) to be taken up in connection with the consideration of the fifth periodic report of the Russian Federation (E/C.12/RUS/5)* (UN Doc No E/C.12/RUS/Q/5/Add.1, 2011) para. 155; and *Strategy for the Implementation of the National Anti-Drug Policy of the Russian Federation in the Period Until 2020* http://stratgap.ru/pages/strategy/3662/4434/4437/index.shtml.

[143] Committee on the Rights of the Child, *General Comment No 13: The right of the child to freedom from all forms of violence*, (UN Doc No CRC/C/GC/13, 2011) para. 37.

use drugs many parts of the world? Or worse, what if a lack of acceptance of drug use translates into violence, the subject matter of article 19?

75. Children whose parents use drugs (or more commonly, alcohol) can be at heightened risk of abuse or neglect. While categorically not accepting any form of physical or mental abuse or neglect while in the care of anyone, regardless of circumstance, what are 'appropriate measures' to protect that child, given the parent's drug dependence? To simply say that drug use by the parent is not acceptable seems unsatisfactory to say the least.

76. The phrase raises many questions and is, therefore, an important normative discussion in the context of article 33. Throughout the remainder of this commentary, the concept of appropriateness is vital and we apply it to various aspects of drug policies. It is therefore important to develop the concept at this early stage. We have identified five core principles:

1. Appropriate measures must be *read in the light of the remaining articles of the CRC*, in particular the General Principles[144] and article 5 (evolving capacities). This is crucial for the development of child rights-based approaches.
2. Appropriate measures *must take into account other provisions more conducive to the realisation of the rights of the child*, brought into play explicitly by article 41(2). Here the highest standard applies. This, in turn, draws in relevant human rights jurisprudence, and requires respect for the rights of others. It also raises the question of the role of the international drug conventions and whether these are conducive to the realisation of the rights of the child.[145]
3. Appropriate measures must address *patterns of vulnerability* including ensuring *gender sensitivity* in programmes and policy responses. This is a core element of rights based approaches. As with many other issues, the impacts on women and girls may be different or differently experienced, and services designed for women and girls will have to address these issues and others that affect women to a greater extent (such as parenting).
4. Appropriate measures must be *evidence-based* and *non-arbitrary*. In other words, they must be based on adequate data, targeted and effective. But it is important to note that effectiveness is not enough. What

---

[144] Art 2 (non-discrimination), art 3 (best interests of the child), art 6 (right to life survival and development) and art 12 (right to be heard and have views taken into account).

[145] For the interplay between these sets of international law see further below paras 91–98 and 159–197.

is appropriate must be effective. But what is effective is not always appropriate.[146] This leads to the fifth principle:

5. Appropriate measures must be *proportionate*. In drug control some rights will inevitably be restricted. But the test for whether such restrictions are lawful is rooted in human rights law. Such measures must be prescribed by law, in pursuit of a legitimate aim and no more than necessary for the achievement of that aim.[147]

With this in mind we may now reframe the two substantive protections in the article as:

Appropriate measures to protect children from the illicit use of narcotic drugs and psychotropic substances as defined in the relevant international treaties

and

Appropriate measures to prevent the use of children in the illicit production and trafficking of such substances

2.2. 'Including Legislative, Administrative, Social and Educational Measures'

77. Legislative, administrative, social and educational measures indicate just how broad ranging the kinds of measures required to address drug use and involvement in the drug trade may be. It is clear from the wording of the article that these measures are directed at both substantive protections. Indeed, we may again reframe the two protections as follows:

Appropriate measures, including legislative, administrative, social and educational measures, to protect children from the illicit use of narcotic drugs and psychotropic substances as defined in the relevant international treaties

and

Appropriate measures, including legislative, administrative, social and educational measures, to prevent the use of children in the illicit production and trafficking of such substances

78. Legislative and administrative measures would include, for example, a national plan of action, legislative change, adequate data collection, appropriate budgeting, governmental co-ordination etc. We have seen above how

---

[146] Executing a child offender will certainly be effective in preventing a repeat offence from that child. It is not, of course, appropriate.

[147] See for example Handyside v UK, *Eur Ct HR*, App No. 5493/72, 1976; and Observer and Guardian v UK, *Eur Ct HR*, App No. 13585/88. 1991.

the Committee on the Rights of the Child has requested much of this information in the specific context of article 33 relating to drug use, where social and educational measures would include, for example, prevention programmes and campaigns, drug education in schools,[148] specialised treatment and rehabilitation, and youth-specific harm reduction programmes.[149] But treatment, rehabilitation and harm reduction programmes have not generally been designed around young people.

79. Poverty and social exclusion, as well as conflict and other factors, can push children towards the drug trade.[150] Children who may be especially vulnerable are those who are street-involved or without adequate parental care. Legislative, administrative, social and educational measures aimed at these root causes are vital. It is important to note also that children may be involved in production and trafficking in myriad ways. It is not all gang-related or urban, and includes farming of illicit crops—most often subsistence farming by families living in extreme poverty. We return to these issues in more detail below.

80. While 'including legislative, administrative, educational and social measures' is very broad, it is notable as much for what is omitted as it is for what is included. The word 'including', indicates that the list is not exhaustive. Indeed, it is clear from the drafting process that rehabilitation and treatment or 'curative measures' were captured by article 33, although this is not specifically mentioned.

---

[148] P. Cuijpers, 'Effective ingredients of school-based drug prevention programs: a systematic review', *Addictive Behaviors*, (2002 (10)) 7–20; P. Cuijpers, R. Jonkers, I, de Weerdt, A. Jong, 'The effect of drug abuse prevention at school: the healthy school and drugs project', *Addiction*, (2002 (97)) 67–73.

[149] See for example, U.S. Institute of Medicine, *Preventing HIV Infection among Injecting Drug Users in High Risk Countries: An Assessment of the Evidence*, September 2006; N. Hunt *A review of the evidence-base for harm reduction approaches to drug use*, London: Report commissioned by Forward Thinking on Drugs—A Release Initiative, 2003; WHO, *Evidence for Action Technical Papers: Effectiveness of Sterile Needle and Syringe Programming in Reducing HIV/AIDS among Injecting Drug Users*, Geneva, World Health Organization 2004; WHO, *Evidence for Action Technical Papers: Effectiveness of drug dependence treatment in HIV prevention*, Geneva, World Health Organization 2004; Canadian HIV-AIDS Legal Network, *Prison Needle Exchange: Lessons from a Comprehensive Review of International Evidence and Experience*, 2004; WHO, *Evidence for Action Technical Papers, Interventions to Address HIV in Prisons: Needle and Syringe Programmes and Decontamination Strategies*, WHO/UNODC/UNAIDS, 2007; WHO, *Evidence for Action Technical Papers, Interventions to Address HIV in Prisons: Drug Dependence Treatments*, WHO/UNODC/UNAIDS, 2007.

[150] See, for example, Yina Paola's story in J. Hunter Bowman 'Real Life on the Frontlines of Colombia's Drug War' in D. Barrett (Ed.) *Children of the Drug War: Perspectives on the Impact of Drug Policies on Young People*, (New York and Amsterdam, International Debate Education Association, iDebate Press, 2011).

81. But let us consider two exclusions to test the limits of this clause: criminal and military. The Committee on the Rights of the Child is consistent in its view that a child who is drug dependent should be seen as a victim, not a criminal.[151] Its most explicit statement in this regard came in February 2011 in relation to Ukraine. The Committee raised concerns that 'legal and attitudinal barriers' may impede access to services for children and that 'new regulations relating to personal possession of drugs may bring more at risk adolescents into contact with the criminal justice system'. It recommended the amendment of laws that 'criminalise children for possession or use of drugs'.[152] Further, articles 37 and 40 give States parties the duty to promote the establishment of specific procedures and institutions dealing specifically with children. Additionally the well known (but not binding) juvenile justice standards establish the principle that detention of juveniles should only be a measure of last resort and for the shortest possible time and promote diversion from the criminal justice system for such children.[153] Hodgkin and Newell in their Implementation Handbook of the CRC are also supportive of this view, referring to harsh penalties on children who use drugs as a 'deeply ineffective form of protection'.[154] This does not exclude criminal justice or law enforcement measures more broadly, but it does *deemphasise* them.

82. From a child rights perspective it is difficult to see how militarised measures to protect children from drug use or to prevent their use in trafficking could be deemed 'appropriate'. Mexico is a current and stark reminder of this. Added to the harms of the drug war already noted above, children have been killed at military checkpoints.[155] In 2010, the Human Rights Committee raised concerns about the use of the military for policing in the country, citing the increased reports of rights violations.[156] The recent announcement of the US to undertake targeted assassinations of suspected drug traffickers in Afghanistan in violation of international humanitarian law is another example. While not specifically related to children it also raises serious questions about the appropriateness of military involvement.[157]

---

[151] O.c. (note 120).

[152] *Concluding Observations: Ukraine*, o.c. (note 63) paras 59 & 60.

[153] *United Nations Standard Minimum rules for the Administration of Juvenile Justice* ('Beijing Rules'), (UN Doc No GA/RES/40/33, 1985), Annex.

[154] R. Hodgkin and P. Newell, 2002, o.c. (note 31).

[155] 'Nineteen in Mexican Army held in deaths of five', *Los Angeles Times*, (5 June 2007); 'Ejército mató a mis hijos: Cynthia Salazar' *El Universal*, (13 April 2010).

[156] Human Rights Committee, *Concluding Observations: Mexico*, o.c. (note 64).

[157] P. Gallahue, 'Targeted Killing of Drug Lords: Traffickers as Members of Armed Opposition Groups and/or Direct Participants in Hostilities', *International Journal on Human Rights and Drug Policy*, Vol. I 2010, pp. 15–33; 'Afghans oppose U.S. hit list of drug traffickers' *Washington Post*,

2.3. *'Protect Children from the Illicit Use'*

83. A question that first arises is whether the article refers to the singular 'child' or the collective 'children'. It is one that is easily answered with reference to article 3, best interests of the child. It is both. Any other conclusion would be nonsensical. Of course State policies will need to look at the situation of children in society, but a child rights based approach requires also consideration of the situations of specific groups and individuals (which relates also to article 2). This applies to both the protection of children from the illicit use of drugs and the prevention of the use of children in illicit production and trafficking.

84. Protection of children from the illicit use of narcotic drugs and psychotropic substances is the first substantive protection in the article (which we have already framed more accurately above). Important to always bear in mind in relation to drug use under article 33 is that *protection* is key. This came through strongly in the drafting process during which earlier submissions from China relating to 'preventing and prohibiting' the child from using drugs were rejected.[158]

85. This leads to a broad reading of the provision in relation to drug use. Throughout policy discussions, however, primary prevention (i.e. stopping the uptake of drug use in the first place) dominates in relation to children and young people.[159] The UN Drug Control Programme's 1998 report 'Youth and drugs: A global overview', referred to already above, is a clear example. Despite its broad title and the various forms of drug use and drug dependence the report discussed, the recommendations were solely about prevention.

86. Two points highlight the broader protection provided by article 33. First, to exclude children currently using drugs would run contrary to the objectives of the CRC (as such article 33 must be read alongside, for example,

---

(24 October 2009); S. Walt 'Afghan drug lords: Targeted until proven innocent' *Foreign Policy*, (11 August 2009).

[158] The original formulation of the article, submitted by China in 1984, though not discussed due to lack of time, was 'preventing and prohibiting the child from using drugs' discussed in the context of then Article 12 on the right to health. In 1986 China suggested a new article 'The States parties to the present Convention shall take measures to prevent and prohibit children from taking drugs'. *Legislative History of the Convention on the Rights of the Child*, o.c. (note 30) pp. 709 & 710.

[159] See for example, *'Youth and Drugs: A global Overview'* o.c. (note 39) and INCB, *Report of the International Narcotics Control Board for 2009*, (UN Doc No E/INCB/2009/1, 2009) (see especially Chapter I: Primary prevention of drug abuse).

article 24). Second, article 33 does not dictate from whose drug use the child should be protected. Upon analysis, this clause in article 33 refers not just to one aspect of protection (i.e. prevention) but *four*:

1. To take appropriate measures to reduce the initiation of drug use by children
2. To take appropriate measures to protect children who are currently using drugs
3. To take appropriate measures to protect children from parental/sibling or other family drug use
4. To take appropriate measures to protect children from drug use in the community

87. We return to these four levels of protection in chapter three. For now it must be pointed out that, in accordance with 'appropriate measures' being non-arbitrary, the protection of children from the illicit use of narcotic drugs and psychotropic substances must take into account contemporary circumstances, best practice and scientific evidence. The CRC is now over two decades old. In those decades much has changed in relation to trends and patterns of drug use and drug dependence among children and young people. Added to this we now have decades of biomedical/psychiatric and psychological research (including on drug dependence), scientific discoveries, research into recreational drug use, experience in drug prevention/health/lifestyle education, harm reduction and years of experience with treatment for drug dependency.

88. When, for example, the discussions on the draft CRC started to gather steam (they had begun in 1978), psychiatrists and psychologists were beginning more and more to distinguish between drug use, problematic use and dependence (especially those professionals basing their classification of substance use on the American Psychiatric Association's Diagnostic and Statistical Manual of mental Disorders, the DSM-IV).[160] Recreational drug use has since become an ever more common aspect of the adolescent experience and most transition out of it without significant health problems.

89. In relation to drug dependence, with new scientific developments and more knowledge on neurological and biological phenomena (such as neurotransmitters, dopamine, DNA and that some people may have a genetic

---

[160] APA, *Diagnostic and Statistical Manual of Mental Disorders, fourth edition (DSM-IV)*, (Washington D.C., American Psychiatric Association, 1994).

vulnerability to addiction), medical-biological aspects[161] have become more of a focus in research. But recently there has been increasing study questioning this medical view and indeed the very concept of 'addiction' itself, with drug dependence being seen as a symptom of damaged environmental, physical, psychological and social well being.[162] We are beginning to understand, for example, that children and young people who have suffered trauma at an early age, and which led to attachment issues, may be at risk as some drugs can generate feelings of attachment.[163]

90. Many drugs now used by children and young people did not exist in 1989. Far fewer children and young people were using drugs. The internet, when the CRC was adopted, was still an experiment. Today, 'legal highs' are widely available for purchase online.[164] Today's world for children is very different in myriad ways. Our reading of article 33 and our consideration of 'appropriate measures' must be able to take this into account.

2.4. 'Narcotic Drugs and Psychotropic Substances As Defined in the Relevant International Treaties'

91. The reference to 'relevant international treaties' requires specific attention as it draws in other branches of international law. Looking at the provision there are two potential roles for the 'relevant international treaties' within article 33, and which we may refer to as *normative* or *subjective*.

92. The *normative* reading of the article indicates that the relevant international treaties set out the kinds of measures envisaged by the CRC that are required to protect children from drugs. Such a reading would be as follows (emphasis added):

> *States parties shall take all appropriate measures, including legislative, administrative, social and educational measures*, to protect children from the illicit use of narcotic drugs and psychotropic substances *as defined in the relevant international treaties* and to prevent the use of children in the illicit production and trafficking of such substances

---

[161] A. I. Lesher, 'Addiction is a brain disease, and it matters', *Science*, (1997 (3)) 278, 45–47.

[162] See for example B. Alexander *The Globalisation of Addiction*, Oxford University Press, 2008.

[163] See, L. J. Cozolino *The neuroscience of human relationships: Attachment and the developing brain* (New York: Norton, 2006).

[164] There are scientific discussions as to whether excessive and compulsive gaming and gambling on line and that compulsive use of the internet are themselves 'addictions'. Dimitri A. Christakis, 'Internet Addiction: A 21st Century Epidemic?' *BMC Medicine*, Vol. 8: 61.

93. The *subjective* reading, on the other hand, indicates that the 'relevant international treaties' refer to the subject matter from which the child should be protected. The relevant treaties are the reference point for the substances being referred to and what qualifies as an 'illicit use' or 'illicit production and trafficking' of those substances. That reading would be:

> States parties shall take all appropriate measures, including legislative, administrative, social and educational measures, to protect children from *the illicit use of narcotic drugs and psychotropic substances as defined in the relevant international treaties* and to prevent the use of children in the illicit production and trafficking of such substances

94. The latter reading is clearly the more logical in the context of the CRC and supported by the drafting history. During the 1986 Working Group which helped to draft the CRC, there was a discussion about which drugs were included. The representative from the Netherlands asked a clarification of the term 'narcotic drugs', suggesting the phrase 'narcotic drugs and psychotropic substances', implying the connection with to the two main drug conventions in force at the time. In this session of the Working Group the suggestion of the delegate from the United States that alcohol be included was rejected.[165]

95. The *subjective* reading of the role of the 'relevant international treaties' within article 33 would also appear to be more in line with the Vienna Convention on the Law of Treaties which provides that 'A treaty shall be interpreted in good faith in accordance with the ordinary meaning to be given to the terms of the treaty in their context and in the light of its object and purpose'.[166] Indeed, if the treaties were intended to define or guide the 'appropriate measures' to be taken, then surely the article would have read '*States parties shall take all appropriate measures, including legislative, administrative, social and educational measures, as defined in the relevant international treaties, to protect children from the illicit use of narcotic drugs and psychotropic substances and to prevent the use of children in the illicit production and trafficking of such substances*'.[167] But this would have had the rather undemocratic effect of binding States parties to the CRC to measures in undefined treaties to which they may not have been parties. When the CRC was drafted the

---

[165] *Legislative History of the Convention on the Rights of the Child*, o.c., (note 30) p. 711.

[166] Vienna Convention on the Law of Treaties, 1155 U.N.T.S. 331, 8 I.L.M. 679, *entered into force* Jan. 27, 1980, Article 31(1).

[167] Alternatively, though considerably less clear, a comma could have been placed before 'as defined in ...' in the original text to separate the treaties from the reference to illicit uses of the substances under control. But this is absent from the official version of the CRC.

1988 trafficking convention had not been adopted and there were far fewer ratifications to both the 1961 and 1971 treaties. There remain today a small number of States parties to the CRC which have not yet ratified the one or more of the drug conventions.

96. This of course does not affect the binding nature of any 'relevant international treaty' in its own right. It simply clarifies their influence on reading article 33 of the CRC. With this in mind, no specific treaties are explicitly referred to. As we will see below, the CRC as framed permits the inclusion of new 'relevant international treaties' as they are adopted or the removal of such treaties as the scope of international drug control may change.

97. As the relevant treaties refer to the substances being referred to, illicit uses of them and illicit production and trafficking, then article 33 cannot be read to capture, for example, morphine for pain relief or methadone for treatment of opiate dependence, as these are medical uses of these drugs protected under the 1961 Single Convention.[168]

98. It should be noted that while article 33 protects from illicit uses, the child should also be protected from negative health outcomes relating to licit uses too under articles 3 (best interests of the child), 6 (right to life, survival and development) and 24 (right to health). For the treatment of Attention-Deficit/Hyperactivity Disorder (ADHD), for example, medications such as methylphenidate (MPH, commonly known in many countries as Ritalin) are prescribed by physicians. It is a practice that has increased in recent years, causing concern in some quarters. The Committee on the Rights of the Child has recently addressed prescription of drugs for the treatment of ADHD in its review of Denmark in 2011 recommending that the State party 'carefully monitor the prescription of psycho-stimulants to children and take initiatives to provide children diagnosed with ADHD and ADD, as well as their parents and teachers, with access to a wider range of psychological, educational and social measures and treatments'.[169] It is an issue the Committee has taken up numerous times in the past.[170]

---

[168] Both are considered essential medicines by the World Health Organisation: *WHO Model List of Essential Medicines*, (Geneva, WHO, March 2009).

[169] Committee on the Rights of the Child, *Concluding Observations: Denmark* (UN Doc No CRC/C/DNK/CO/4, 2011) para. 52.

[170] See *Concluding Observations: Australia* (UN Doc No CRC/C/15/Add.268, 2005) para. 49; *Finland* (UN Doc No CRC/C/15/Add.272, 2005) para. 38; *Japan* (UN Doc No CRC/C/JPN/CO/3, 2010), para. 60; *Norway* (UN Doc No CRC/C/NOR/CO/4, 2010) paras 42 & 43; *Belgium* (UN Doc No CRC/C/BEL/CO/3-4, 2010) paras 58 & 59.

2.5. 'Prevent the Use of Children in the Illicit Production and Trafficking of Such Substances'

99. Appropriate measures to prevent the use of children in the illicit production and trafficking in drugs is the second substantive protection in article 33 (which we have set out more accurately above). This element of article 33 is closely related to article 32 on freedom from economic exploitation. There is a difference in wording from the first substantive protection—i.e. 'prevent' rather than 'protect'. It is a more pointed reference. As noted above, protection from the illicit use of narcotic drugs and psychotropic substances requires a broad reading, and results in four levels of protection. Preventing the use of children in the illicit production and traffic of these substances is more specific.

100. It is clear that, firstly, States parties must take appropriate measures to prevent the use of children in the illicit *production* of the substances covered by the relevant international treaties. This would appear to cover both farming in relation to controlled crops, or industrial cultivation, whether on a large or small scale (e.g. hydroponic cannabis production). The Committee on the Rights of the Child has, in the past, raised concerns about the use of children in coca farming in Colombia.[171] It would also cover the process of producing organic substances from those plants or the production of synthetic substances. The article does not cover, however, *licit* production of controlled substances, such as the production of opium poppy for morphine supply. But such work could be captured by ILO 182 and the CRC (article 32) if it were dangerous or likely to damage health, education, development etc. Its illicit status in this regard is not relevant. To be captured by article 33, however, being 'illicit' is necessary.

101. Secondly, *trafficking* is covered. The use of children as mules or direct involvement in armed violence would surely also be captured. While buying and selling on a small scale is not referred to, it would not be in keeping with a child protection and rights-based approach if the use of children in any form of criminality were to be permissible. Indeed, this second clause of article 33 is a rather broad ranging protection from involvement in criminality applied specifically to the relevant substances under international control. It may capture a whole range of activities, even if minor of themselves.[172]

---

[171] *Concluding Observations: Colombia*, o.c. (note 112) paras 82, 83, 88.
[172] See *1988 Commentary* o.c. (note 55) p. 92, para. 3.121.

102. While drug use and dependence among children is dealt with under basic health and welfare by the Committee and closely connected with article 24 (right to health), the prevention of children in the production and the use in trafficking is seen as a measure of special protection—i.e. a form of exploitation or abuse.[173] As the clause is framed around prevention the situation of children in fact involved in the drug trade is not explicitly referred to. They are, of course, not excluded from the protection of the CRC. Again we see the clear need to read article 33 in the context of the CRC as a whole. In relation to children involved in the drug trade, articles 19 (freedom from neglect or violence) 39 (reintegration of victims) and 40 (juvenile justice) are of particular relevance.

3. Commentary on the Text

3.1. First Substantive Protection: Four Levels of Protection of Children from the Illicit Use of Narcotic Drugs and Psychotropic Substances

3.1.a Appropriate Measures to Reduce the Initiation of Drug Use by Children

103. States parties must work to address initiation of drug use by children. This obligation is relatively self-evident. But it is one that must be read in the context of 'progressive realisation' for the purposes of article 4 (implementation of the rights in the Convention).[174] It is not possible to prevent all drug use—either immediately or even in the long term. The State must, however, take measures to progressively reduce the numbers of young people initiating drug use. This is far more readily measurable than a simple statement of 'ending' or 'preventing' drug use, and certainly more realistic.

104. Indicators (and benchmarks) and data collection are, as always, important, particularly if progress is to be measured. At a global level, however, limited surveillance from many of the world's most populous nations makes it impossible to accurately estimate the total number of drug-involved young people.[175] For the information we do have, data collection methods

---

[173] Committee on the Rights of the Child, *CRC Treaty specific reporting guidelines, Harmonised according to the common core document*, (UN Doc No CRC/C/58/Rev.2, 2010), para. 39(c)(ii).

[174] Committee on the Rights of the Child, General Comment No. 5 *General Measures of Implementation of the Convention on the Rights of the Child* (UN Doc No CRC/GC/2003/5, 2003), para. 7.

[175] C. Cook and A. Fletcher 'Youth drug use research and the missing pieces in the puzzle: How can researchers support the next generation of harm reduction approaches?' in: D. Barrett (ed.) *Children of the Drug War: Perspectives on the Impact of Drug Policies on Young People*, (New York and Amsterdam, International Debate Education Association, iDebate Press, 2011).

are imperfect. For the most part studies examining the prevalence of drug use among young people rely on self-reporting from an accessible group of young people, normally school students. However, the fear of a lack of anonymity, or of potential repercussions for an admittance of drug use may bias results due to under-reporting. A recent American study comparing data collected via self-completion questionnaires with biological markers found that teenagers' hair specimens were 52 times more likely to identify cocaine use than their self-reporting of drug use behaviours.[176] In addition, school based surveys do not capture those not attending school, while home based surveys fail to capture those living on the streets—two key indicators of risk for drug dependence and drug related harm.

105. While prevention measures must be adopted, they too must be 'appropriate' and should be directed by child rights considerations. We now know that universal prevention programmes are not effective (though a lot of children may be reached by them). In addition, many prevention programmes are not audited sufficiently to gauge effectiveness. Researchers from South Africa have recently studied youth-focused prevention programmes in the country and reported that 'most prevention programmes are not guided by evidence-based practices and are implemented in the absence of evidence of their effectiveness'.[177] On the other hand, a recent randomised controlled trial from the UK suggested that brief, personality-targeted interventions can prevent the onset and escalation of substance misuse in high-risk adolescents.[178] Family and environmental factors must also be fully taken into account.

Three further examples help to illustrate the need for child rights scrutiny of prevention measures:

Schools

106. It is clear and uncontroversial that States parties must take educational measures, which would include school based drug education and public information campaigns. But how should schools tackle drug use? Random school drug testing (often as part of a 'zero tolerance' policy) has been employed

---

[176] Delaney-Black V., et al. 'Just Say "I Don't": Lack of Concordance Between Teen Report and Biological Measures of Drug Use' *Pediatrics*, (2010 (126)) 5, 887–893.

[177] N. Burnhaus, B. Myers and C. Perry, 'To what extent do youth-focused prevention programmes reflect evidence-based practices? Findings from an audit of alcohol and other drug prevention programmes in Cape Town, South Africa', *African Journal of Drug and Alcohol Studies* (2009 (8))1, 1–8.

[178] P. J. Conrod et al. 'Brief, personality-targeted coping skills interventions and survival as a non-drug user over a 2-year period during adolescence' *Archives of General Psychiatry*, 2010 Jan.; 67(1): 85–93.

in various countries as a prevention measure. It is one which seems on the face of it acceptable, but upon analysis through a child rights framework is problematic on a number of grounds. Firstly, its effectiveness is highly questionable. A large scale study in the US involving over 400 schools and 75,000 students showed no deterrent effect of such testing.[179] Secondly, the child's right to privacy is rarely a consideration (article 16), and refusal of consent can lead to disciplinary measures including exclusion from school. Indeed, efficacy and the right to privacy are connected. If the measure is ineffective then the interference with the child's privacy must be considered 'arbitrary' for the purposes of article 16. Meanwhile, the best interests of the tested child does not appear to be a primary consideration—or at least, it is unclear how this test is applied beyond the obvious (that it is not in a child's best interests to use drugs). Labelling of a child as a 'drug user' can have negative impacts on education and psychological wellbeing[180] while drug tests fail to distinguish between recreational drug use (which would not require treatment intervention) and problematic use or dependence.

107. The CRC shows us that, regardless of the problem, it is important to keep treating all children with respect and dignity. Invasive searches of children for drugs, however, raise serious concerns relating to privacy and dignity. In the US a 13 year old student, Savana Redding, was strip searched based on a tip from another student that she had brought Ibuprofen (a legal prescription or over-the-counter drug) to school. No drugs were found under Savana's clothes after two female school officials searched her underwear. The Juvenile Law Center argued that strip searching the 13 year old girl violated international norms of dignity and respect.[181] Savana's case is a landmark in the United States.[182] The majority of the Supreme Court found that searching Savana had been unreasonable and violated her rights under the fourth amendment of the US Constitution.[183]

---

[179] R. Yamaguchi, et al., 'Relationship between student illicit drug use and school drug-testing policies', *Journal of School Health*, (2003 (73)) 159–164.

[180] C. Bonell, A. Fletcher, 'Addressing the wider determinants of problematic drug use: advantages of whole-population over targeted interventions', *International Journal of Drug Policy*, (2008 (19)) 267–269.

[181] Brief of Juvenile Law Center, et al., as Amici Curae in Support of Respondent, No. 08-479. *Stafford Unified School District#1, et al., Petitioners v. April Redding, Respondent* (2009) 557 US. No. 08-479.

[182] Supreme Court of the United States, *Stafford Unified School District#1, et al., Petitioners v. April Redding, Respondent* (2009) 557 US. No. 08-479.

[183] 'The right of the people to be secure in their persons, houses, papers, and effects, against unreasonable searches and seizures, shall not be violated, and no Warrants shall issue, but

108. Police searches of children's backpacks and clothes are common in Brazil and frequently result in abuses. In 2007, a child rights NGO from Rio de Janeiro, Projeto Legal, filed a petition on behalf of children living in the *favela* of Vigário Geral who were subjected to embarrassing invasions of their privacy during police searches.[184] The organisation alleged that the searches violated the constitutionally recognised rights of the child to freedom and privacy and claimed that it was not part of public security authorities' powers to create and implement policies aiming at children, especially when in a situation of great vulnerability.[185] As part of Mexico's war on drugs the '*Mochila segura*' (Safe schoolbag) programme has consisted of a series of police led random searches of schoolbags. Human rights groups have raised concerns about the impact on education.[186]

Public Campaigns

109. From a child rights perspective and in order to be effective (and therefore appropriate) the messages conveyed in prevention campaigns must be accurate and objective. This has been a consistent recommendation of the Committee. Further, if article 12 is taken into account then children and young people should be involved in the development of such messages. Indeed, poorly developed prevention campaigns can be harmful. According to the UN Drug Control Programme in 1999 'There is an openness among youth to information, if it is factual and does not contrast too sharply with their personal experience of drugs. Scare tactics used in some information material do not serve the purpose for which they are intended, but rather significantly reduce the trust that youth may have in the advice of adults and in some case even encourage risky behaviours'.[187] It should go without saying that such campaigns should not serve to stigmatise children or to degrade them. Compare this to a

---

upon probable cause, supported by Oath or affirmation, and particularly describing the place to be searched, and the persons or things to be seized.

[184] Carlos Nicodemos, *Advogando pelos Direitos Humanos dos Adolescentes no Sistema Socioeducativo: Dez Casos Exemplares de Enfrentamento às Violações de Direitos Humanos dos Adolescentes Autores de Ato Infracional* (Rio de Janeiro: Secretaria Especial de Direitos Humanos, 2007), 85.

[185] M. Gueraldi 'Young soldiers in Brazil's drug war' in D. Barrett (ed.) *Children of the Drug War: Perspectives on the Impact of Drug Policies on Young People*, New York and Amsterdam, International Debate Education Association, iDebate Press, 2011.

[186] Claudia Bolaños, 'CDHDF se opone a Programa Mochila Segura'. El Universal, 28 May 2010.

[187] '*Youth and Drugs: A Global Overview*' o.c. (note 39).

recent Russian anti-drug campaign in which children and adolescents were depicted eating human faeces, being raped, and looking at photographs of mutilated bodies.[188]

Laws and Policies

110. Legislative preventive measures must also be scrutinised from a child rights perspective. Many countries have adopted 'aiding and abetting', 'encouragement' or 'incitement' laws which apply higher criminal penalties for those considered to be facilitating drug use among children. In Ukraine for example, this is punishable by five to twelve years in prison.[189] This does not seem on the face of it to be problematic. The intention is to protect children from being targeted for sales or from being exploited. It has been noted by the Committee on the Rights of the Child without concern[190] and is included in the advice on implementation of the CRC by Hodgkin and Newell.[191] But these laws are in fact problematic in a significant way that affects the rights of the child; they fail to include safeguards for harm reduction services. The result, seen in some countries, is that service providers (providing, for example, sterile injecting equipment as a HIV prevention measure) fear prosecution and are reluctant to assist.[192] Such services not only protect drug using young people from immediate harms (article 24), but are also sources of information (article 13) and gateways to social services (articles 26 and 39). Indeed, these laws may inhibit the creation of youth specific harm reduction services, a requirement of article 33 as confirmed recently by the Committee.[193] Such laws must include specific safeguards for drug treatment and harm reduction services if they are to be deemed 'appropriate' for the purposes of article 33. Otherwise they may fail to protect children who are using drugs.

---

[188] 'Sex, drugs and excrement smear the screen in Russian anti-drug campaign' The Moscow News, 1 December 2010.

[189] Article 315 *Criminal Code of Ukraine* 'Inducement to use narcotics, psychotropic substances or their analogues'.

[190] See for example: Committee on the Rights of the Child, *Concluding Observations: Slovakia*, (UN Doc No CRC/C/SVK/CO/2, 2007) para. 65.

[191] R. Hodgkin and P. Newell, o.c. (note 31) p. 503.

[192] See, *Young people and injecting drug use in selected countries of Central and Eastern Europe*, o.c. (note 13).

[193] O.c. (note 63).

3.1.b *Appropriate Measures to Protect Children Currently Using Drugs*

111. To exclude children currently using drugs from any reading of article 33 would seem nonsensical and contrary to the adopted wording. While protecting a child from the illicit use of drugs clearly denotes prevention, if a child is using drugs then protecting a child from 'the illicit use' must involve also (as appropriate, in the best interests of the child, and respecting their views and evolving capacities) policies and interventions to protect them from the negative health, education and social harms associated with such use. This is crucial because for children who are using drugs, primary prevention means nothing and has, by definition, not worked, or has not reached them.

112. During the drafting of the CRC it was clear that prevention was foremost in the minds of the drafters, but this cannot be assumed to imply a hierarchy, as if prevention is more important than addressing current drug use among children. Indeed, such an interpretation may result in discrimination against drug using children if the rights and needs of those that do not currently use drugs were deemed to take precedence. These levels of protection must be given equal weight.

113. Treatment and rehabilitation or curative measures were also discussed during the drafting process,[194] although it did not result in stressing in the CRC the importance of adequate treatment. The Committee on the Rights of the Child has, however, consistently recommended such measures.[195] The acceptance of protection for children who currently use drugs places article 33 in line with contemporary jurisprudence on the right to health, principles relating to deprivation of liberty and juvenile justice,[196] and, clearly, the fact that in periodic reporting the Committee on the Rights of the Child now addresses this aspect of article 33 under the 'disability, basic health and welfare' cluster of rights.[197]

114. The 1961 Single Convention on Narcotic Drugs (article 38) and the 1971 Convention on Psychotropic Substances (article 20) both contain an

---

[194] *Legislative History of the Convention on the Rights of the Child* o.c. (note 30) 710, at the recommendation of the Ad Hoc NGO Group.

[195] O.c. (note 121).

[196] 'The Beijing Rules', o.c. (note 153). Rule 26.6 highlights the importance of drug dependence treatment.

[197] Committee on the Rights of the Child, *CRC Treaty specific reporting guidelines, Harmonised according to the common core document*, (UN Doc No CRC/C/58/Rev.2, 2010) para. 34(f).

obligation on States parties to provide treatment for drug dependence. We explore below what this obligation might mean read in the light of the CRC.

Drug Dependence

115. If a child or adolescent develops problematic drug using behaviours or drug dependence, then the right to treatment must be recognised even if article 33 is not explicit on this point. Specialised drug treatment for young people is multi-faceted. As described by the UK organisation DrugScope, it can include 'residential rehabilitation, substitute prescribing and needle exchange for a small minority, through to services that offer a combination of 'motivational', 'psychosocial' and 'harm reduction' interventions for the majority.'[198] There are now evidence based therapies developed for adolescents which involve parents. Multidimensional Family Therapy (MDFT) developed by Prof. Howard Liddle from the Center for Treatment Research on Adolescent Drug Abuse at the University of Miami is an example of good practice, now applied in many places in the world.[199] The MDFT therapist works separately with the adolescent and together with him or her, the parents and the school. The results have been promising.

116. There are also programmes connected to the criminal justice system. In several countries Juvenile Drug Courts have been established. The aim of most of these special courts is to facilitate early identification of young offenders with drug problems, divert them from incarceration and to reduce the time of delivery of treatment for these young people.[200] Drug courts,

---

[198] *Young people's drug and alcohol treatment and the crossroads: What it's for, where it's at and how to make it even better*, London, DrugScope, 2010, p. 25.

[199] H. A. Liddle, *Multidimensional Family Therapy for Adolescent Drug Abuse: Clinician's Manual*, (Center City, M.N. 2009, Hazelden Publishing Co.); H. A. Liddle, *Multidimensional; Family Therapy: A 12-weeks intensive outpatient treatment for adolescent cannabis users*, (Washington DC, Center for Substance Abuse Treatment, 2000).

[200] C. Cooper, *Juvenile drug court programs* (Washington DC, 2001, US Department of Justice, Office of Justice Programs, Office of Juvenile Justice and Delinquency Prevention, 2001) NCJ No. 184744; C. M. McGee et al., 'Applying drug court concepts in the juvenile and family court environments: A primer for judges' (on line: http://www.ametrican.edu; R. J. Kimbrough, 'Treating juvenile substance abuse: The promise of juvenile drug courts', *Journal of the Office of Juvenile Justice and Delinquency Prevention* (2001 (5)) 2, 11–19; Bureau of Justice Assistance, *Juvenile Drug Courts Strategies in Practice, Monograph*, (Washington DC, US Department of Justice, May 2003); Office of Justice Programs, *Drug Court Clearinghouse and Technical Assistance: Juvenile Drug Court Update*) (Washington DC, American University, School of Public Affairs and the Office of Justice Programs Drug Court Clearinghouse and Technical Assistance Project, 2001); M. Roberts, J. Brophy and C. Cooper, *The Juvenile Drug Court Movement, Fact Sheet*, (Washington DC, US Department of Justice, Office of Justice programs, Office of Juvenile Justice and Delinquency Prevention, 1997). In some cases intensive multidimensional family treatment

however, have had mixed results and human rights and due process concerns have been raised.[201]

117. Drug treatment must be appropriate for children and young people, and here many other articles in the CRC are of direct relevance, in particular article 24. Treatment services should recognise the different patterns of use and initiation among girls (e.g. initiation via sexual partners). Existing adult (and often male oriented) services may not be appropriate. Residential places in adult facilities may not be safe environments, for example, and adult services (whether in- or out-patient) may not address patterns of drug use among younger people (i.e. type of drug and methods of consumption). In addition, many young people may not identify with older users. States parties must ensure treatment for young people 'to the maximum extent of available resources' (article 4). While specialised drug treatment can be expensive, a recent UK study found that the 'immediate benefits of treatment (i.e. until young people reach the age of 18) are sufficiently large alone to offset the cost of providing the treatment. Added to this, the long term benefits of treatment (in terms of improved employment prospects and reduced likelihood or become an adult problematic drug or alcohol user) further increase the ratio of benefits to costs'.[202] In the UK, Government spending on these services went up from £15.3 million in 2003/4 to £24.7 million in 2007–08, with numbers in treatment increasing from 17,001 in 2005/6 to 23,905 in 2007/8 and 24,053 in 2008/9.[203]

Recreational Drug Use

118. It is important to make a clear distinction between recreational drug use, problematic drug use and drug dependence (although the latter is a form of problematic use). The reasons for drug use among young people are many, complex and debated,[204] but the assumption underpinning most

---

programme is integrated in a day treatment program, which the Drug Court orders the child to participate in.

[201] See for example, *Drug courts are not the answer: Toward a health centered approach tod rug use* (Drug Policy Alliance, New York, 2011).

[202] 'Specialist drug and alcohol services for young people—a cost benefit analysis' London: Department for Education, Research report DFE-RR087, 2011.

[203] DrugScope o.c. (note 198) p. 22.

[204] M. Bredgen et al., 'Deviant friends and early adolescents' emotional and behavioural adjustment,' *Journal of Research on Adolescence* (2000 (10)) 2, 173–189; J. Brooks-Gunn, 'Do neighbourhoods influence child and adolescent development?' *American Journal of Sociology* (1993 (99)) 2, 353–395; W. Downs and L. Harrison, 'Childhood maltreatment and the risk of substance problems in later life', *Health and Social Care in the Community* (1998 (6)) 1, 35–45; D. Elliott et al., 'The effects of neighbourhood disadvantage on adolescent development',

governments responses to drug use is that it is in all cases aberrant or deviant behaviour, and always harmful, always a threat. But while children
should be protected from illicit drug use, and while drug use among young
people can be an indicator of later problems (or current ones),[205] experi-
menting with drugs has become increasingly common among young people,
and most young people who experiment with drugs or use them recreationally do not develop serious drug problems.[206]

119. Not all children who use drugs need treatment. Indeed, this is the case
with the vast majority of young people who use drugs occasionally or recreationally. This was not acknowledged or discussed during the drafting process, but is not impeded by the CRC as framed. While such use is still 'illicit',
if the reality of the situation is not accepted, then the policies and interventions adopted will not be appropriately targeted and evidence based in
order to protect these young people. Simply put, measures that focus on
the worst case scenario fail to speak to the lived experiences of many recreational users. A young person using ecstasy on occasional weekends, for
example, may not be in need of dependence treatment. And he or she may
not be experiencing or have experienced any adverse consequences. But the
risks are there. For example, he or she may not be aware of what, exactly
their pill contains. For this reason services such as Bouman Mental Health
Services in the Netherlands offer testing facilities which inform users of
what they have bought. Such services are, however, controversial and illegal
in many countries, seen as 'promoting' drug use. Recreational users may be
encouraged to cease use over time, but in the meantime, the possible harms
associated with ecstasy use can be mitigated.[207]

Journal of research in Crime and Delinquency (1996 (33)) 4, 389–426; K. A. Maxwell, 'The role of
peer influence across adolescent risk behaviours', *Journal of Youth and Adolescence* (2002 (31))
4, 267–277; G. F. Koob, L. Le Moal, 'Addiction and the Brain Antireward System', *Annu. Rev.
Psychol.* (2008 (59)) 29–53; N. D. Volkow et al., 'The addicted brain: insight from imaging studies', *J. Clin. Invest.* (2003(111) 1444–1451. F. Measham and M. Shiner, 'The legacy of 'normalisa-
tion': The role of classical and contemporary criminological theory in understanding young
people's drug use', *International Journal of Drug Policy*, (2009 (20)) 6, 502–508.

[205] J. H. Beitchman, et al., 'Comorbidity of psychiatric and substance use disorders in late
adolescence: A cluster analytic approach', *American Journal of Drug and Alcohol Abuse* (2001
(27)) 3, 421–440.

[206] European Monitoring Centre on Drug and Drug Addiction, *Drug use amongst vulnerable young people: Prevention strategies need to target young people most at risk* (Lisbon, EMCDDA,
2003).

[207] See for example www.drugscope.org.uk/resources/drugsearch/drugsearchpages/
dancesafety.htm.

120. One of the most significant of drug-related harms, is coming into contact with the criminal justice system, leading many to call for drug law reform (including the recent high level Global Commission on Drug Policy, which included Kofi Annan, Louise Arbour and many former Presidents). The International Narcotics Control Board, however, sees no room for tolerance on this, criticising law reform aimed at decriminalising possession for personal use in some countries. The Committee on the Rights of the Child has yet to address recreational drug use, such as club drug use, and the various harm reduction measures that can mitigate the risks associated with it. Would the Committee on the Rights of the Child encourage a more tolerant approach if this is conducive to the fulfilment of the right to health? It appears so. In its Concluding Observations on Ukraine, the Committee explicitly called for the decriminalisation of children who use or possess drugs.[208] But far more discussion must be had by the Committee on this topic.

Holistic Approach

121. Connecting prevention, life style training, treatment and harm reduction is the need for a holistic approach to drug use among children and young people, supported by a child rights framework. For the most part, problematic drug use is associated with a range of underlying issues such as mental health, family problems including inter-generational drug dependence, self-esteem and so on. This is relevant not only to treating people for drug dependence, but to harm reduction and prevention too. A recent study from Ireland illustrates the point.[209] Eighty-six young people under the age of nineteen and using opiates were interviewed about their drug use and life situations. Connecting the findings to relevant articles of the CRC we see the holistic approach emerging: forty-four had injected opiates, with eighteen being hepatitis C positive (articles 6, 24). Forty-five had undergone previous psychiatric treatment (article 24). Seventeen had deliberately overdosed, fourteen of them girls (articles 24 and article 2). Twenty-six had been homeless in the last months (article 27). The majority had experienced sibling or parental alcohol or opiate use (articles 18, 19 and 27). Forty-one had past convictions (articles 37 and 40). But perhaps the most instructive finding was related to education. Of the eighty-six young people interviewed only five were currently in school (article 28). This may seem obvious, as someone

---

[208] O.c. (note para. 60(b)).
[209] J. Fagan et al. 'Opiate-dependent adolescents in Ireland: a descriptive study at treatment entry' *Irish Journal of Psychological Medicine*, 25 (2). pp. 46–51.

using opiates may well end up excluded due to their drug use. But in fact 49% initiated heroin use after leaving school, indicating that school retention may have an important role in prevention.[210] The role of recreation (article 31) is also vital. Sheer boredom and a lack of opportunities for recreational activity has a role in initiation into drug use.[211]

122. The need for holistic approaches is also evident in relation to drugs and poverty. IRIN (the humanitarian news and analysis service of the UN Office for the Coordination of Humanitarian Affairs) has reported that some young women in Afghanistan give their children opium to eat to keep them quiet or when they are in pain.[212] A recent report on UK television documented the use of opium as a hunger suppressant because it was simply cheaper than food.[213] The report shows how opium dependence among rural women has been exacerbated by the lack of availability of health services and lack access due to cultural restrictions. It is an issue that has recently been taken up by the CRC Committee.[214]

3.1.c   *Appropriate Measures to Protect Children from Drug Use in the Family*

123. States parties are required to protect children from use within the family. That this is required by article 33 is consistent with the recommendations in the Committee's General Comment No. 7 (on implementing child rights in early childhood)[215] and recent Concluding Observations.[216] Moreover, article 33, as drafted, does not specify from whose drug use the child should be protected.

---

[210] From the same country see also, for example J. M. Hayes and G. O'Reilly 'Emotional intelligence, mental health and juvenile delinquency' (Cork: Juvenile Mental Health Matters, 2007). See also National Advisory Committee on Drugs (NACD) and Drug and Alcohol Information and Research Unit (DAIRU) *Drug Use in Ireland and Northern Ireland; First results from the 2006/2007 Drug Prevalence Study*, (Dublin, NACD and DAIRU, 2008).

[211] See for example, J. MacIntosh et al. 'The reasons why children in their pre and early teenage years do or do not use illegal drugs' *International Journal of Drug Policy*, Vol. 16, Issue 4, (2005) pp. 254–261.

[212] IRIN, *Afghanistan: Opium eases my pain, keeps my children quiet; women use opium not for fun or luxury, but as the only available painkiler to them, said Mahbooba Ebadi, an obstetrician in Balkh* (Kabul, IRIN, 16 July 2009).

[213] 'Unreported World,' episode 12: 'Opium diet', *Channel 4*, 2010.

[214] *Concluding Observations: Afghanistan*, 2011 o.c. (note 120) para. 51(d).

[215] Committee on the Rights of the Child, *General Comment no. 7: Implementing child rights in early childhood*, (UN Doc No CRC/C/GC/7, 2005).

[216] For example, *Concluding Observations: Sweden*, 2009 o.c. (note 35) paras 48 & 49; and *New Zealand* o.c. (note 126) paras 31 & 32.

124. That children should be protected from drug use within the family is also consistent with the place of the family within the CRC[217] and the central role which the drafters recognised parents play in helping their children realise their rights. Here we focus on parental drug use and dependence but recognise of course the potential impact on children when siblings or other family members are experiencing drug problems.

Prenatal Care for Mothers Who Use Drugs

125. Article 24 of the CRC includes the right to prenatal care, requiring that States parties shall take appropriate measures 'to ensure appropriate prenatal and postnatal healthcare for mothers'.[218] This should be read alongside article 33, and, indeed, the preamble requiring special protection for children due to their 'physical and mental immaturity'.

126. The influence of stress, drinking, smoking and using drugs during pregnancy is becoming increasingly clear[219] as are the potentially irreversible effects on foetuses.[220] Many children suffer the first days of their life from neonatal abstinence syndrome. This raises a difficult question: how can the negative effects on the developing foetus be minimised?

127. It must be made very clear that many women who use drugs and are pregnant will often want to seek assistance. A major barrier to this is fear of coming into contact with law enforcement or stigma and discrimination relating to their drug use or dependence. The Irish Women's Health Council has noted that '[T]here is still a double standard that judges women's substance misuse more harshly than men's, particularly if the woman has children. This greater stigma can result in greater guilt and shame for women and for their families, and may lead to women being reluctant to seek treatment.'[221] There is also the fear of losing their child. Consensual and supportive approaches are available in some countries, such as drug liaison

---

[217] Articles 5 (describing responsibilities of parents), 7 (the right, as far as possible, to be cared for by the parents), 18 (parents' joint responsibility assisted by the State).

[218] See also B. Abrahamson, *Violence Against Babies: Protection of Pre- and Post-natal Child Rights, under the Framework of the Convention on the Rights of the Child,* (Utah, World Family Policy Center, 2005).

[219] For example, H. El Marroun, et al., 'Intrauterine Cannabis Exposure Affects Fetus growth Trajectories: The Generation R- Study', *Child and Adolescent Psychiatry* (2009 (48)) 12, 1173–1181.

[220] For example, S. L. Leech, et al., 'Prenatal substance exposure: Effects on attention and impulsivity of 6 years olds', *Neurotoxcology and Teratology,* (1999 (21)) 2, 109–118.

[221] Women's Health Council, *Women & Substance Misuse in Ireland: Overview* (undated) p. 6 http://www.drugsandalcohol.ie/12439/1/womenSubstanceOverview.pdf.

midwives who can assist drug using women who are pregnant.[222] Voluntary, community-based drug treatment services also play an important role.[223] Substitution therapy (e.g. with methadone or buprenorphine) is also recommended for pregnant opiate users.[224] Studies have shown that methadone exposure is, however, associated with adverse perinatal outcomes[225] (though likely less than if the mother continued using street heroin). Specialised care for pregnant women who are prescribed methadone and their babies is therefore required.

128. What is the appropriate response, however, when a pregnant woman does not want to cooperate with an outpatient clinic or treatment? In certain circumstances, juvenile judges in the Netherlands may take action by appointing a guardian over the child which is not yet born.[226] A mother may also be admitted to a psychiatric ward where medical and psychiatric treatment may be given. (This, of course, requires concrete human rights safeguards, such as clinical assessments, second opinions, and regular reviews).[227]

129. It is certainly a difficult practical and ethical area. A recent UNICEF report puts the challenge succinctly: 'to change the attitude of both society and health-care professionals so that these women are treated as 'pregnant women who have a problem of drug use' and who need to be treated with dignity and respect, rather than just 'drug users who happen to be pregnant', with all that this implies'.[228]

---

[222] F. Macrory, 'The drug liaison midwife: developing a model of maternity service for drug-using women', in: Hilary Klee, Marcia Jackson and Suzan Lewis, editors, *Drug Misuse and Motherhood*, (London, Routledge, 2002) 234–249.

[223] S. Ruben and T. Fitzgerald, 'The role of drug services for pregnant users: the Liverpool approach', in: H. Klee, M. Jackson and S. Lewis, (eds), *Drug Misuse and Motherhood* (London, Roudledge, 2002) 224–238.

[224] United Nations Office on Drug Control. Substance abuse treatment and care for women: case studies and lessons learned. United Nations, New York, 2004.

[225] For example, B. Cleary et al. 'Methadone and perinatal outcomes: a retrospective cohort study' *American Journal of Obstetrics and Gynacology*, 2011 Feb.; 204(2): 139.e1–9.

[226] For instance the Court in Groningen on 10 October 2008, *LJN: BG4372* (decision on the appoinment of a guardian to an unborn foetus and decision to place the child out of home after birth).

[227] For example, *UN Principles for the protection of persons with mental illness and the improvement of mental health care*' (UN Doc No GA/RES/46/119, 1991) Annex.

[228] UNICEF, *Blame and Banishment: The Underground HIV epidemic affecting children in eastern Europe and Central Asia* (New York, UNICEF, 2010) 46. See also: UNICEF, *Children at Risk of Contracting HIV/AIDS in Afghanistan* (New York, UNICEF December 2008). See further Eurasian Harm Reduction Network 'Women in Drug Policy' (Vilnius: EHRN, 2010) p. 5.

Children of Drug Using Parents

130. Parental drug use and dependence can have considerable impacts on children.[229] Some children become caregivers—caring for parents no longer capable or temporarily incapable of caring for themselves. Some ignore their own needs in the process and can go through a mourning process if the health of the parent is deteriorating. There might be loss of earning capacity of the parent which can have a profound effect on the daily life of the child, including basics such as food and education. Inter-generational drug dependence is also a considerable concern and some children can be exposed to domestic violence related to drugs and alcohol. Indeed, the harms that many children suffer due to parental drug and alcohol dependence are clear.[230] But we must again ask: what are 'appropriate measures' to protect these children?

131. Custody is an important debate. It is not the case that removing a child from a parent who uses drugs is in each case an 'appropriate measure' to protect that child, nor is it always in the child's best interests. Not all people who use drugs are dependent, and not all people who are drug dependent are causing their children significant harm. In some countries, people who use drugs are entered onto official registries. These registries can form the basis for challenging custody. In Kyrgyzstan, for example, where an estimated 25% of injecting drug users are women, article 147 of the Family Code makes chronic drug dependence the basis for loss of custody.[231]

---

[229] M. Barnard and J. Barlow, 'Discovering Parental Drug Dependence: Silence and Disclosure', *Children's Society*, (2003(17)) 1, 45–46; D. Forester and J. Harwin, 'Parental substance misuse and child welfare: outcomes for children two years after referral', *British Journal of Social Work* (2009 (38)) 8, 1518–1538; D. Hogan and L. Higgins, *When parents use drugs; key findings from a study of children in the care of drug-using parents* (Dublin, Trinity College, 1997); J. L. Johnson and M. Left, 'Children of substance abusers: overview of research findings', *Pediatrics* (1999 (103)) 5 Supplement, 1085–1099.

[230] A. Bancroft, S. Wilson, S. Cunningham-Burley, K. Backett-Milburn and H. *Parental drug and alcohol misuse:Resilience and transition among young people* (York, 2004, the Joseph Rowntree Foundation as part of the Drug and Alcohol series); Advisory Council on Misuse of Drugs, *Hidden Harm: Responding to the needs of children of problem drug users*; Report of an Inquiry (London, Advisory Council on the Misuse of Drugs, 2003); ACMD, *Hidden Harm: Responding to the Needs of Children of Problem Drug Users* (London, Advisory Council for the Misuse of drugs, 2003); Scottish Executive, *Getting Our Priorities Right* (Edinburgh, Scottish executive, 2003); D. Forrester and J. Harwin (2006) 'Parental substance misuse and child care social work: findings from the first stage of a study of 100 families' *Child and Family Social Work*, 11(4) November, pp. 325–335; A. Wales et al. 'Untold damage: Children's' accounts of living with harmful parental drinking', *Scottish Health Action on Alcohol Problems*, 2009; M. Barnard. and J. Barlow, 'Discovering parental drug dependence: Silence and disclosure', *Children and Society*, (2003 (17)) 1, 45–56.

[231] EHRN 'Women in Drug Policy' o.c. (note 228) pp. 3–4.

132. Each case must be taken on its own circumstances, and while removal from custody may be required in the child's best interests, and is sometimes requested by struggling parents, other options are available. For example, the provision of methadone or buprenorphine to an opiate dependent parent may assist in enabling them to stabilise their drug use and focus on parenting. Focused social work geared towards improving parenting skills and fostering family cohesion has shown to be promising.[232] This in turn could contribute towards the rendering of 'appropriate assistance to parents and legal guardians in the performance of their child-rearing responsibilities' for the purposes of article 18(2). The Committee on the Rights of the Child has made clear the need to support families experiencing drug or alcohol dependence.[233]

133. Contrary to this, however, are laws or policies that deny or remove such assistance. A UK government white paper released in December 2010, for example, included stripping social welfare benefits from people who refuse drug dependence treatment. Children's organisations raised fears about the impact on dependent children.[234]

134. Mobilizing social support[235] for children of drug using parents is, of course, vital, as there is a risk, for example, of mood and anxiety disorders.[236] The stigma attached to these children and the shame they may feel can be great. Group work (face-to-face groups) with adolescents and young children of drug users has shown to be helpful.[237] Through such groups children from socially isolated families can learn that there are others with similar experiences. There is, however, the other side of the equation, where policies or practices may discriminate against children of drug using parents

---

[232] See for example See D. Forrester et al. *Happiness project working with resistance in families experiencing violence: Option 2—Cardiff and Vale—Evaluation report 2008*, (Prepared for the Welsh Assembly Government, UK, 2009); and S. Dawe and P. Hartnett 'Reducing potential for child abuse among methadone-maintained parents: results from a randomized controlled trial' *Journal of Substance Abuse Treatment* 2007, 32(4): 381–90.

[233] See for example, *Concluding Observations: New Zealand* o.c. (note 126).

[234] The Children's Society, *The Children's Society's response to the publication of the White Paper—Reducing Demand, Restricting Supply, Building Recovery*, (London, The Children's Society, 9 December 2010).

[235] Hoefnagels, C., Meesters, C. and Simenon, J., 'Social support as predictor of psychopathology in the adolescent offspring of psychiatric patients', *Journal of Child and Family Studies* (2007 (16)) 1, 87–97.

[236] J. Johnson et al., 'Evidence of depression in children of substance abusers', *International Journal of the Addictions* (1990 (25)) 4 A, 465–479.

[237] Neta Peleg-Oren, 'Group intervention for children of drug-addicted parents using expressive techniques', *Clinical Social Work* (2002(30)) 4, 403–418.

(article 2). Women who use drugs in Kyrgyzstan, for example, have reported that schools refused to accept their children (article 28).[238]

3.1.d   *Appropriate Measures to Protect Children from Drug Use in the Community*

135. There can be no doubt that children are affected by drug use in their communities, including related health, economic and crime concerns. Children are also confronted with drug-related violence. That States parties are required to protect children from the illicit use of drugs in their communities may relate, for example, to the child having the right to a safe environment within which to develop (article 6). Public health based interventions such as harm reduction programmes to improve public health and reduce crime may therefore be considered important in this context. This is particularly so when such programmes have community-wide benefits, such as those seen in relation to North America's only safe injection facility— 'Insite' in Vancouver, Canada.[239]

136. More broadly, and bearing in mind our introduction on children as justification in drug control, it should be noted that drug control laws and policies aimed at reducing supply of and demand for narcotic drugs and psychotropic substances are supported by article 33. But two important qualifications must be made:

1.   *Such Measures Must Be Subject to Human Rights and Child Rights Scrutiny*

137. Supply and demand reduction, particularly in relation to law enforcement and sentencing must be approached carefully as without the 'appropriate measures' limitation it could be read to justify anything. The measures taken must conform to the principles outlined above in order to qualify as 'appropriate'. Importantly, they must be shown to progress towards the four levels of protection outlined above.

---

[238] Dzhalbieva ID, Ermolaeva IV and Tokombaeva MM, 'Limited Access to Services and Socio-psychological Factors Influencing the Spread of HIV Among Women IDUs in the Southern Region of Kyrgyzstan. Report on Research Results'. Bishkek: Asteria Foundation, 2009, *cited in* EHRN, Women and Drug Policy o.c. (note 228) p. 3.

[239] For references to the many studies evaluating Insite, including systematic reviews and cohort studies, see 'Insight into Insite', BC Center for Excellence in HIV/AIDS, 24 March 2009, http://www.aidslex.org/site_documents/DR-0099E.pdf; and http://supervisedinjection.vch .ca/research/.

138. The rights of others, of course, must be taken into account. Yet human rights abuses in the context of supply and demand reduction are well known.

- Drug crackdowns have resulted in extra-judicial killings, including of children.[240]
- Police violence against people who use drugs is widespread[241] and the use of withdrawal as a means to extort money and to coerce testimony has been documented.[242]
- During his 2007 mission to Indonesia, the UN Special Rapporteur on Torture, Manfred Nowak, found many cases of torture to extract information from drug suspects and a disproportionate number of prisoners incarcerated for drug offences.[243] An EU-US funded maximum security prison intended for terror suspects instead housed mostly drug suspects, many on death row.[244] In 2008 to mark UN day against drugs, June 26th, two Nigerians were taken on a day's notice from the prison, tied to with tyre tubes to makeshift wooden crosses, and shot with M-16 rifles.[245]
- Each year China executes dozens of people on June 26th, executions which are widely reported.[246] Annually, the death penalty for drugs results in as many as 1,000 executions.[247]
- Although the government denies it, there are credible stories indicating that Iran executes children for carrying and supplying drugs, with some detained until they turn eighteen when they will be executed.[248]

[240] Human Rights Watch, *Not Enough Graves, the War on Drugs, HIV/AIDS and Human Rights Violations* (New York, Human Rights Watch, 2002) [on the situation in Thailand].

[241] J. Csete, *Do Not Cross; Policy and HIV Risk Faced by People Who Use Drugs* (Toronto, Canadian HIV/AIDS Legal Network, 2007). T. Rhodes, L. Platt, A. Sarang et al., 'Street Policing, Injecting drug use and Harm Reduction in a Russian City: A Qualitative Study of Police Perspectives', *Journal of Urban Health*, (2006(89)) 5, 911.

[242] Human Rights Watch, *Rhetoric and Risk, Human Rights Approaches Impeding Ukraine's Fight Against HIV/AIDS* (New York, Human Rights Watch, 2006).

[243] *Report of the Special Rapporteur on torture and other cruel, inhuman or degrading treatment or punishment, Manfred Nowak: Mission to Indonesia*, (UN Doc No A/HRC/7/3/Add.7, 2008).

[244] Ibid., para. 96.

[245] 'Nigerians executed in Indonesia' *BBC News*, (27 June 2008). A catholic priest, Fr. Charlie Burrows, who witnessed the executions, described them as torture. 'Priest relives firing squad deaths for court' *Sydney Morning Herald* (19 September 2008).

[246] For example, Xinhua News Agency, *China executes drug traffickers in south China*, 26 June 2010 (referring to nine executions); Xinhua News Agency, *China executes six drug dealers*, 27 June 2008; Associated Press: *China executes 64 to mark UN anti-drugs day*, 27 June 2002.

[247] P. Gallahue and R. Lines *The Death Penalty for Drug Offences: Global Overview 2010*, (London, Harm Reduction International, 2010).

[248] Amnesty International, *Iran the last executioner of children* (London, 2007).

- Judicial corporal punishment is applied for drug taking (and alcohol consumption) in many countries.[249]
- Hundreds of thousands of people, including those under eighteen, are detained in drug detention facilities in China, Viet Nam, Cambodia and other countries (particularly in East Asia)—without due process and subject to forced labour, beatings, denial of meals and other abuses.[250]
- In February 2011, Thailand announced plans to round up and forcibly 'treat' up to 30,000 people identified as people who use drugs. This would be carried out through the establishment of temporary detention centres, many run by the civil-defence forces.[251]
- Women drug mules or women convicted of non-violent drug related offences are incarcerated in disproportionate numbers, with no account being taken of the needs of their dependent children, who, with no other options available, are often incarcerated with them.[252]
- Prison populations worldwide have skyrocketed due to drug control laws and policies. Poorer people and those from ethnic minorities are disproportionately represented. Human Rights Watch has documented considerable racial disparities in drug law enforcement and sentencing in the US.[253]

139. Child rights and human rights scrutiny applies also to the interpretation of the international drug conventions under which UN member states have agreed broad measures of supply and demand reduction. These measures represent the current international consensus on supply and demand reduction relating to the substances they control. On a basic level, however,

---

[249] These include Singapore, Malaysia, Iran, Yemen, Saudi Arabia, Qatar, Brunei Darussalam, Maldives, Indonesia (Aceh), Nigeria (northern states), Libya and United Arab Emirates (UAE).

[250] B. Doherty, 'Raped, beaten, killed: Cambodians fate at illegal internment camp funded by UN', *The Guardian* (29 October 2010); Open Society Institute (OSI) *Detention as treatment: detention of methamphetamine users in Cambodia, Laos and Thailand* (New York, 2010); *Skin on the cable* o.c. (note 25); Joseph Amon, 'Who will defend the Children in Cambodian Drug Rehab Centres?', *The Nation*, (March 31, 2010).

[251] 'Human rights NGOs to Thai Government—Do not repeat history!' *The Nation*, 22 February 2011. Following widespread civil society and international condemnation, the campaign did not go ahead as planned.

[252] Celso Athayade and MV Bill, *Mulheres e o tráfico* (Rio de Janeiro, Objetiva, 2007) in Portuguese. See also J. Fleetwood and A. Torres 'Mothers and Children of the Drug War: A View from a Women's Prison in Quito, Ecuador' in D. Barrett (ed.) *Children of the Drug War: Perspectives on the Impact of Drug Policies on Young People*, New York and Amsterdam, International Debate Education Association, iDebate Press, 2011.

[253] Human Rights Watch, *Targeting blacks: drug law enforcement and race in the United States Human Rights* (New York, Human Rights Watch, 2008).

these treaties cannot be interpreted so as to interfere with the rights of the child or human rights more broadly. The Indonesian Constitutional Court, for example, has looked to the 1988 trafficking convention to justify the death penalty, comparing drug trafficking to crimes against humanity.[254]

2. The Policy Paradigm to Be Adopted and the Exact Measures to Be Put in Place Are Not Set Out in the CRC

140. It is clear from article 33 that no specific measures are set out. Moreover, the only paradigm represented in the CRC is child rights. The CRC is open on the policy paradigm to be adopted (we explain this in more detail below) and the measures to be put in place to protect children from the illicit use of narcotic drugs and psychotropic substances so long as they are 'appropriate'. Here we refer again to the four principles already set out above.

141. While it is certainly arguable that article 33 may support the current prohibitionist/law enforcement-based system as a form of protection from drugs, equally arguable is that harm reduction as a paradigm constitutes 'appropriate measures' in terms of protecting children from drug use in the wider community, or that legal regulation and control of all currently illicit drugs as a policy option may be an appropriate measure for such protection. It is an open debate. Health, human rights and drug policy organisations have called for an 'impact assessment' of global drug control efforts to inform it moving forward. A child rights impact assessment would, of course, be a welcome inclusion in any such analysis.[255] In the context of aerial fumigation of coca in Colombia, the Committee on the Rights of the Child has already made such a call.[256]

3.2. *Second Substantive Protection: Appropriate Measures to Prevent the Use of Children in the Illicit Production and Trafficking of Such Substances*

142. Children and young people may be used in the drug trade for many reasons—because they agree to work for lower wages than adults, for example, or because and if they are arrested they will cycle out of the criminal justice

---

[254] Edith Yunita Sianturi, Rani Andriani (Melisa Aprilia), Myuran Sukumaran, Andrew Chan, Scott Anthony Rush 2–3/PUU-V/2007 [2007] IDCC 16 (30 October 2007) pp. 100–101.

[255] Transform Drug Policy Foundation 'Time for an impact assessment of drug policy' http://www.tdpf.org.uk/Impactassessmentlead.htm.

[256] *Concluding Observations: Colombia* o.c. (note 112) para. 72.

system faster.[257] Criminals may also exploit the minimum age of criminal responsibility as younger children would not be subject to heavy criminal penalties. In other words, the risks to the trafficker are less. It is clear that there is an obligation on States parties to prevent the use of children in the illicit production and trafficking of narcotic drugs and psychotropic substances. But what are 'appropriate measures' to do so?

3.2.a *Appropriate Measures to Prevent the Use of Children in Illicit Production and Trafficking*

143. The year before the CRC was adopted a resolution was adopted in the General Assembly which focused on the use of children in the illicit traffic in narcotic drugs.[258] The resolution stated that the General Assembly 'was alarmed by the fact that drug dealer's organisations are making use of children in their illicit production and of trafficking in drugs...' and in strong terms condemned those criminal activities which involve children 'in the use, production and illicit sale of narcotic drugs and psychotropic substances'. The resolution called upon States to join together to establish national and international programmes to protect children from involvement in illicit production and trafficking (as the then draft Convention on the Rights of the Child had done). It also called for 'suitable severe punishment of drug-trafficking crimes that involve children'.

144. It seems relatively straightforward that as a form of exploitation, the use of children in this or any other form of criminality should be established as a crime (this was suggested for explicit inclusion in the article by China, but rejected).[259] But from a child rights perspective this is not enough. It is of doubtful deterrent effect, and prosecuting offenders does little for the root causes—it is reactive.

145. Another resolution was adopted by the General Assembly of the UN two years later which requested the Secretary-General and member States

---

[257] S. Leviton et al., 'African-American Youth: Drug Trafficking and the Justice System', *Pediatrics* (1994 (93)) 65 Suppl. 1078–1084. See also: J. N. Okundaye, 'Drug Trafficking and Urban African American Youth: Risk Factors and PTSD', *Child and Adolescent Social Work Journal* (2004 (32)) 3, 285–302.

[258] General Assembly resolution 43/121, *Resolution on the use of children in the illicit taffic in narcotic drugs and rehabilitation of drug-addicted minors* (A/RES/43/121, 1988).

[259] China's 1986 proposal included 'appropriate criminal punishment, to anyone who uses or incites a child to become involved in various forms of drug trafficking'. See: *Legislative History of the Convention n the Rights of the Child*, o.c. (note 30) 710, 711.

to undertake research and analysis of the phenomenon of the instrumental use by adults of children in profit-making criminal activities.[260] Since then, however, little work has been done on children involved in the drug trade and systematic data collection is lacking (although extremely difficult to collect in this context). Experience and testimony from the few research data we could locate shows that children and young people become involved in the drug trade for myriad reasons, key among them poverty, drug dependence, homelessness and a lack of other options.[261] The NGO 'Watchlist on children and armed conflict' reports (quoting sources from UNAMA) that in Afghanistan 'in their drive to acquire more drugs, some children join criminal networks or armed groups'.[262]

146. A documentary from 2006, produced by Brazilian hip-hop artist MV Bill entitled *Falcão: meninos do tráfico*,[263] documented the lives of seventeen boys working in the drug trade in the country's favelas. Their stories reveal the reasons that lead them into crime as well as the violence perpetrated and suffered by them due to their activities. One boy explained: '*I'm no outlaw... I don't want to see my mother suffering*'. Another boy explained the influence of his own drug dependence: '*I do not get sad about anything. I'm always drugging myself. I am a thief. I rob because no one gives me anything... I have to rob. I rob to live.*' When asked what he wanted to be when he grew up, another boy said '*Outlaw. Because it makes money and helps. Hell is where we are... Here we live the reality, where there are bullets everywhere and the law is the worst possible. My mother already has three dead children*'. Indeed, by the end of the research, all but one of these seventeen boys was dead having never reached eighteen.[264]

147. A recent study from Canada, meanwhile, showed that the majority of a cohort (n=529) of street involved young people (aged 14–26) reported

---

[260] General Assembly resolution 45/115, *Resolution on the instrumental use of children in criminal activities*, (UN Doc No A/RES/45/115, 1990).

[261] Peer pressure, image and basic profiteering may also be a factor. In the context of drug dealing on US college campuses see A. Rafik Mohamed and Erik D. Fritsvold, *Dorm Room Dealers: Drugs and the Privileges of Race and Class*, (Boulder, CO, Lynne Reinner Publishers, 2009). Boredom, lack of leisure options and social outlets may also be a factor for some young people and does away with the stereotype that dealing in drugs is something for the poor.

[262] Watchlist on Children and Armed Conflict, *Setting the Rights Priorities: Protecting Children by Armed Conflict in Afghanistan*, (New York, Watchlist, June 2010) 21.

[263] An accompanying book is available in Portuguese, MV Bill *Falcao: Meninos Do Trafico*, (Rio de Janeiro, Objetiva, 2006) (in Portuguese).

[264] The documentary is recounted in M. Gueraldi 'Young soldiers in Brazil's drug war' in D. Barrett (ed.) *Children of the Drug War: Perspectives on the Impact of Drug Policies on Young People*, New York and Amsterdam, International Debate Education Association, iDebate Press, 2011.

dealing drugs. They were more likely to be crack cocaine users and homeless, and to be motivated by drug dependence and basic survival needs.[265] Here, we see clearly the connection between the two substantive protections in article 33.

148. As such, for the purposes of article 33, social and educational measures must be considered 'appropriate' for preventing the use of children in production and trafficking, targeting the root causes of such involvement. Articles 26, 27 and 28 are clearly related. The CRC requires adequate budgets for such measures pursuant to article 4. The vast majority of funds spent in drug control in many countries, however, are still spent on law enforcement and interdiction measures.

149. Finally, as noted above, while measures should be taken to prevent the use of children in the drug trade, the CRC Committee is clear that children should also not be used in the fight against drug trafficking.[266] In our view this should extend to using children as police informants.

3.2.b *Appropriate Measures Relating to Children Suspected of or in Fact Involved in Illicit Production and Trafficking*

150. Article 33 does not explicitly refer to children involved in the drug trade. It is broad in its reach but is focused predominantly on the 'use' of children in the drug trade. It is therefore directed at those who may exploit the child. But it is not always the case that a child is coerced in this way. It is important to distinguish between the ways in which children may be involved in the drug trade. Many young people may be involved, for example, in low level dealing that may be unconnected to this form of coercion. The reason to make this distinction, as with the distinction between types of drug use, is to ensure that responses are appropriate and targeted. A middle class adolescent dealing drugs in order buy expensive aspirational products,[267] for example, is not the same as a street involved child selling drugs to survive[268]

[265] D. Werb et al. 'Risks Surrounding Drug Trade Involvement Among Street-Involved Youth', *The American Journal of Drug and Alcohol Abuse*, 34: 810–820, 2008.

[266] *Concluding Observations: Mexico (OPAC)* o.c. (note 18).

[267] A. Rafik Mohamed and E. Fritsvold o.c. (note 262).

[268] Werb et al. o.c. (note 265).

or a child working her family's opium plantation,[269] who in turn is not the same as a child soldier in Rio[270] or a young member of a gang in Honduras.[271]

151. It should go without saying that, as with drug use, juvenile justice principles (article 40) must apply to children involved in the drug trade. While the drug trade, as a form of criminality, may be focused on in the CRC, this does not justify stricter sanctions applied to drug related crimes. Unfortunately, in many countries drug related crimes are considered more serious than others.

152. If the *use* of children in the drug trade is in question and is seen as a form of *exploitation*, then the use of criminal sanctions at all must be very carefully considered even if the child is above the minimum age of criminal responsibility. As noted recently by the International Labour Office 'In IPEC's[272] Balkans project, 'significant attempts have been made in Bulgaria to achieve legislative coherence that decriminalizes children who, engaged in illicit activities, are victims of the worst forms of child labour'.[273]

153. Many other articles of the CRC are, of course, relevant here. In relation to policing, for example, articles 16 and 37 would protect against invasions of privacy (e.g. invasive searches) and police abuse. Unfortunately, when tackling drugs and organised crime, human rights can be easily cast aside. The Canadian cohort study cited above observed heightened levels of police violence against street involved young people involved in the drug trade.[274] During his mission to Indonesia in 2007, the UN Special Rapporteur on Torture reported that 'After having inspected the cells, the Special Rapporteur ran into Mohammed Tasroni, aged 17, from Jakarta, who was handcuffed to a chair in an office belonging to the drug unit on the fourth floor. Mr. Tasroni was in the process of being interrogated by Mr. Sudartianta (No. 65080313) and had very strong swellings on this face as well as other traces of recent

---

[269] Hunter-Bowman o.c. (note 150).

[270] L. Dowdney o.c. (note 13).

[271] See for example, F. Martin and J. Parry-Williams, *The Right Not to Lose Hope: Children in conflict with the law, a policy analysis and examples of good practice. A contribution to the UN Study on Violence Against Children from the International Save the Children Alliance* (London, Save the Children, 2005).

[272] International Programme on the Elimination of Child Labour http://www.ilo.org/ipec/lang--en/index.htm.

[273] 'Accerating action against child labour: Global report under the follow-up to the ILO Declaration on Fundamental Principles and Rights at Work 2010' (International Labour Office, Geneva: 2010) para. 269.

[274] D. Werb o.c. (note 265).

beatings all over his body.'[275] Article 39, meanwhile, relates to the rehabilitation and reintegration of child victims. This includes both victims of the drug trade, young people who are street involved and/or drug dependence, and victims of police violence or institutional violence.

154. The ILO has called for better linkages between criminal justice systems and child labour efforts using ILO Convention 182 as a mechanism.[276]

3.2.c   *Involvement in the Illicit Production and Trafficking of Drugs As a Worst Form of Child Labour*

155. Article 3(c) of ILO Convention 182 (1999) Concerning the Prohibition and Immediate Action for the Elimination of the Worst Forms of Child Labour, defines 'the use, procuring or offering of a child for illicit activities, in particular for the production and trafficking of drugs as defined in the relevant international treaties' as a worst form of child labour. It clearly borrows from the language of article 33, and singles out production and trafficking, but is broader as it covers also other illicit activities. It should be fairly straightforward that the use of a child (or the child's involvement even if not coerced) in illegal activities must be considered a worst for of child labour. It clearly qualifies as 'hazardous labour' (often seen as a proxy measurement for the worst forms), as it may adversely affect the child's health, safety or development.[277] It may also expose children to violence, incarceration or worse.[278] Moreover, as with child labour more broadly, many children are involved in the agricultural side of the drug trade, often as unpaid family workers. Agriculture may account for 70% of all child labour worldwide and is considered to be one of the most dangerous sectors in which to work, formally or informally.[279] On top of the existing harms associated with agricultural work,[280] children involved in production of illicit crops are also exposed to armed violence and crop eradication campaigns.

---

[275] Special Rapporteur on torture and other cruel, inhuman or degrading treatment or punishment, o.c. (note 243) para. 141.

[276] 'Accelerating action against child labour' o.c. (note 273) para. 270.

[277] Ibid., p. 6.

[278] It was estimated that sixteen children in 2007 were on death row in Iran for trafficking drugs across the Iran-Afghanistan border. 'Afghanistan: Paper fears child drug smugglers face hanging in Iran', *BBC News*, 4 October 2007.

[279] For an overview see the International Programme on the Elimination of Child Labour (IPEC) http://www.ilo.org/ipec/areas/Agriculture/lang--en/.

[280] See for example, Human Rights Watch, *Fingers to the bone: United States failure to protect child farm workers* (New York, Human Rights Watch, 2000).

156. It is the status of illegality that renders *all* involvement with the drug trade a worst form of child labour. This is recognised by ILO 182, prefacing article 3(c) with 'illicit activities' and the fact that licit production and trade is not covered under article 3(c) or article 33. This begs the hypothetical question: What if the legal status of currently illicit substances (or some of them) were to change? What if, in time, marijuana, coca or opium poppy, for example, were not under international control? What would this mean for this category of worst forms of child labour?

157. Involvement in the production and trade in these, now licit, substances, would cease to be a worst form of child labour in law *prima facie*. Instead, the question would relate to the actual conditions involved as with all other forms of child labour. So long as it was not dangerous or damaging to health and therefore captured by art 3(d) of ILO 182, or indeed, harmful from a broader child rights perspective and caught by art 32 of the CRC, such involvement would not, it seems, be considered a worst form of child labour. This would be a qualitative analysis, depending on the specific tasks, hours, equipment, chemicals, conditions, age appropriateness etc., rather than a blanket label. At present all involvement in the drug trade is categorised as a worst form of child labour. But how would we categorise different roles if the legal situation were different? What would constitute 'children in employment' versus 'children in child labour' versus 'hazardous work by children'.[281] Consider, for example, a child of sixteen working part time in her parents' shop and selling tobacco. Compare this to a child of nine working full time on a legal tobacco plantation.[282]

158. While this is merely a thought experiment at this stage, it is an important one and worth further discussion.[283] The reason to single out illicit production and trafficking in drugs in ILO 182, and in article 33, was the criminal nature of such activities, and the associated violence and risks to any children involved. Where, then, is the *source* of the harm requiring this definition of a category of worst form of child labour? We must note that it is

---

[281] 'Accelerating action against child labour' o.c (note 273), p. 6.

[282] In the context of tobacco farming, regardless of the legality of the product, see Gamlin, J. Romo, P. Diaz, Hesketh, T. 'Exposure of young children working in Mexican tobacco plantations to organophosphorous and carbamic pesticides, indicated by cholinesterase depression', in *Child Care, Health and Development* (2007) May 33 (3) 246–248. See also Human Rights Watch, *Hellish Work: Tobacco workers in Kazakhstan*, (New York, Human Rights Watch, 2010).

[283] See Report of the Global Commission on Drug Policy, 2011, available at http://www.globalcommissionondrugs.org/Report; see also 'Count the Costs: 50 years of the war on drugs', a multi-NGO campaign to mark the fiftieth anniversary of the 1961 single Convention on Narcotic Drugs www.countthecosts.org.

now well established that the prohibition of these crops and substances has created the macroeconomic criminal market in drugs that now surrounds this work. This has brought with it violence, corruption and destabilisation.[284] As such, ongoing debates around the creation of a new system of legal regulation of production and supply of currently illicit substances in order to reduce associated criminality and violence are pertinent here. Could a new policy paradigm better protect children involved in the drug trade by changing the nature of the trade itself?

3.3. What Are the 'Relevant International Treaties' and Which Drugs Are Captured by Article 33?

159. As we have seen above, 'relevant international treaties' are those that identify the substances covered under article 33 and identify what an illicit use of them might be. But which ones are they, and which drugs are therefore included?

3.3.a International Drug Conventions

160. The first question that must be answered is whether the three international drug conventions are, indeed, 'relevant international treaties' for the purposes of article 33. The question is simply answered in the affirmative. During the drafting process the World Health Organization explicitly stated that the relevant international treaties were the 1961 Single Convention and the 1971 Psychotropics Convention.[285] These treaties schedule hundreds of 'narcotic drugs and psychotropic substances', for the purposes of article 33.[286] These two treaties clearly qualify.

161. The 1988 Trafficking Convention had not been adopted when the CRC was being drafted, however, and the draft of the 1988 Convention was also never referred to, so the situation in this regard is not so clear cut. The 1988 Convention schedules precursor chemicals rather than narcotic drugs

---

[284] This is recognised within the UN system. See *Making drug control fit for purpose: Building on the UNGASS decade. A report by the Executive Director*, UN Doc No E/CN.7/2008/CRP.17, (March 2008) 10. See also UNDP, *Human development report 2003*, Chapter 13 on Colombia, 'Taking narcotics out of the conflict: the war on drugs'.

[285] This was already in the period of the technical review of the Convention on the Rights of the Child in 1989, when the Working Group determined which recommendations to accept. See UN Doc No E/CN.4/1989/WG.1/CRP.1, p. 37. See also, *Legislative History of the Convention on the Rights of the Child*, o.c. (note 30) pp. 709–712.

[286] For the lists of scheduled substances see (narcotic drugs) http://www.incb.org/pdf/forms/yellow_list/48thedYL_Dec_08E.pdf; and (psychotropic substances) http://www.incb.org/pdf/e/list/green.pdf.

and psychotropic substances, although some such chemicals are also consumed, such as ephedrine.[287] It would appear to make sense that the 1988 Convention is now also a 'relevant international treaty', despite its adoption in the years after the drafting process (but just prior to the adoption of the CRC). Its inclusion in article 33 requires the recognition that the Convention on the Rights of the Child is open to changes in the international framework of drug control, through the creation of new treaties and through older ones being superseded. This is consistent with the wording of the article which does not refer to any individual treaty explicitly.

162. The scope of control of the drug conventions is consistently developing with new substances being added to the lists under each treaty at sessions of the Commission on Narcotic Drugs. As they are added, these substances are captured by article 33. And as they are removed, they are simultaneously removed from the scope of article 33.

3.3.b   WHO Framework Convention on Tobacco Control

163. Nicotine is a highly addictive drug, and cigarette smoking (the most popular nicotine delivery method, but which must be disaggregated from nicotine itself which is not carcinogenic) results in millions of preventable deaths every year. It is a considerable public health concern, including among children.

164. At the time of drafting the CRC there was no international treaty on tobacco. But as the case of the 1988 Convention shows, the CRC is open to new treaties being included. Today the WHO Framework Convention on Tobacco Control has 172 States parties. It would appear that, like the 1988 Convention, the FCTC is today a 'relevant international treaty' for the purposes of article 33, especially considering its specific reference to the CRC in its preamble.

165. This means that tobacco is equated with other dangerous drugs in article 33, but it is significant that it is not controlled under the Framework Convention in the same way as those substances scheduled under the 1961, 1971 and 1988 drug treaties. Rather, the Framework Convention adopts a public health-based approach to tobacco control, and does not prohibit its sale, transport or possession. Instead, the Framework Convention imposes a system of legal regulation and control with specific protections for

---

[287] The full list is available at http://www.incb.org/pdf/e/list/red.pdf.

children (or 'minors'). Protection from the 'illicit use' of tobacco remains important, as use under the age limit at which tobacco products may be purchased remains illicit for the purposes of the FCTC.

166. Another significance of this is that if the FCTC were considered a relevant international treaty, article 33 would capture the involvement of children in the illicit tobacco trade—itself large scale and dangerous. But this would be regardless of the conditions of work. Its illicit status would be sufficient to be captured. Art 15 of the FCTC covers this aspect of the tobacco trade and a draft protocol on this is in process,[288] while illicit tobacco production and trafficking is already covered by article 3(c) of ILO 182.[289]

3.3.c Alcohol

167. Alcohol is not captured.[290] As noted above, the US suggested its inclusion during the drafting process and this was not taken up. This does not mean it could not in future come under article 33. But it requires an international treaty on alcohol which at present does not exist.

168. In 2006 the American Public Health Association adopted a resolution entitled 'A call for a Framework Convention on Alcohol Control'.[291] The APHA wanted to draw lessons from the tobacco movement and the Framework Convention on Tobacco Control. In 2009 at an inter-country consultation in New Delhi representatives from south east Asian countries took up again the issue of an alcohol control treaty,[292] but it seems that a new WHO Convention on alcohol is not one around which many are rallying to create.

---

[288] The fourth session of the Intergovernmental Negotiating Body (INB4) on a Protocol on Illicit Trade in Tobacco Products was held from 14 to 21 March 2010 in Geneva. The session decided to recommend to the Conference of the Parties to consider, at its fourth session, the draft protocol to eliminate illicit trade in tobacco products contained in document FCTC/COP/INB-IT/4/7, in accordance with decisions FCTC/COP2(12) and FCTC/COP3(6). http://www.who.int/fctc/inb/inb4/en/index.html.

[289] Licit tobacco production, on the other hand, may be caught by art 3(d) but this depends on actual conditions rather than its legal status.

[290] Despite the fact that this particular drug is leading contributor to the global burden of disease and premature death. See World Health Organization, *Global strategy to reduce the harmful use of alcohol*, (Geneva, 2010).

[291] American Public health Association, *Statement: A Call for a Framework Convention on Alcohol Control* (APHA Governing Council, Washington DC, 2006).

[292] World Health Organization, *Possibility of Developing a Framework Convention of Harm of Alcohol Use; Report of an Intercountry Consultation* (New Delhi, WHO Regional office for South east Asia, 2009).

169. With what we know of the damage that alcohol can cause to young people, it is a significant omission.[293] It should be borne in mind, too, that alcohol is widely connected to poly-drug use among young people, particularly in recreational settings, and is easily obtained at low prices and without proof of age by young people in many countries. The potential for harm is also likely to be greatest when young people use both drugs and alcohol.

3.3.d Solvents

170. Solvents such as glue and aerosols[294] are not included despite their significant usage by young people. Some solvents are, however, scheduled under the 1988 Convention, and others have been the subject of resolutions at the Commission on Narcotic Drugs.[295] Both alcohol and solvents (to a lesser extent) are often dealt with by the Committee on the Rights of the Child in its Concluding Observations in the context of adolescent health.[296]

3.3.e The CRC and the Policy Paradigm for Drug Control

171. Within drug policy discussions, some tend to place article 33 alongside the three international drug conventions, as if it were part of the same system of control (an unusual role for a human rights treaty).[297] An important question that therefore arises is whether the CRC could sustain a move towards a model of legal regulation and control of currently illicit drugs, i.e. an entire change of direction for these substances. Looking at our analysis so far the question has already been answered. The CRC is open on the broad policy paradigm adopted. Two specific findings lead us to this conclusion:

172. First, we discussed above the role of the 'relevant international treaties' within the CRC and that, as worded, the CRC does not allow for the

---

[293] C. A. Essau and D. Hutchinson, 'Alcohol use, Abuse and Dependence', in: C. A. Essau, editor, *Adolescent Addiction: Epidemiology, Assessment and Treatment* (Amsterdam, Boston, London, Academic Press, 2009) 61–116.

[294] http://www.emcdda.europa.eu/publications/drug-profiles/volatile.

[295] Commission on Narcotic Drugs, *Use of 'poppers' as an emerging trend in drug abuse in some regions'* CND resolution 53/13, (UN Doc No E/2010/28, 2010) p. 35.

[296] On solvents, such as glue and petrol, see for example, Concluding Observations: Central African Republic (UN Doc No CRC/C/15/ADD.138, 2000) para. 80; Greece, (UN Doc No CRC/C/15/ADD.170, 2002) para. 74; Bangladesh (UN Doc No CRC/C/BGD/CO/4, 2009) para. 65. On alcohol see *Belarus* (UN Doc No CRC/C/BLR/CO/3-4 2011), para. 59; *Serbia* (UN Doc No CRC/C/SRB/CO/1, 2008) para. 56; *Ireland* (UN Doc No CRC/C/IRL/CO/2, 2006) para. 51.

[297] See, for example, 'Declaration of the World Federation Against Drugs', 2008.

relevant international treaties to dictate its normative content. This of course does not undermine the legally binding nature of the drug conventions themselves (which enjoy near universal ratification), but indicates that the CRC is not tied up with their terms.

173. Second, we have seen how the CRC allows for new treaties to be included as 'relevant international treaties' as new substances come under international control. It also allows for their removal. The inclusion of the FCTC is especially significant. The Framework Convention adopts a public health-based approach to tobacco control, and does not prohibit its sale, transport or possession. Instead, the Framework Convention imposes a system of legal regulation and control with specific protections for children (or 'minors').

174. This shows that the framework of the drug conventions does not represent the only way to protect children from harmful drugs, rather they reflect the current international consensus around specific substances. As such, no specific approach to drugs adopted in other treaties is explicitly enshrined in the CRC. This is appropriate, leaving room for change to the international drug control framework and developing scientific evidence.

175. If new treaties may be included within the 'relevant international treaties', then old or obsolete treaties, or those that have been superseded, may be removed. Such changes would not be fatal to art 33 (or art 3(c) of ILO 182 for that matter) thereby requiring amendment or rendering these provisions redundant. Rather, the substances captured would change, as would the definition of an 'illicit use' (taking into account age restrictions that may be adopted in a legally regulated market). The need for protection from the illicit use of substances would therefore remain. Moreover, as some form of illicit production and trafficking in currently licit substances (e.g. tobacco) would surely continue, the protection afforded by article 33 would not disappear for children used in this form of illicit activity. The same conclusion must therefore apply to transport, sales and so on.

176. What this suggests is that article 33 is no barrier to moving from a prohibitionist system to one of legal regulation and control provided that States parties: continue to live up to the four protections identified above in the context of drug use; continue to work to prevent the use of children in any remaining criminal market in regulated substances; and continue to protect children from harmful, hazardous work (regardless of form). Indeed, it seems that there is little argument that a model of legal regulation and control could not be an 'appropriate measure' for the purposes of

article 33.[298] A full, rights based, evaluation and impact assessment whereby current approaches are assessed alongside a range of alternatives would assist in investigating this option.

3.4. *Interpreting the UN Drug Conventions Alongside the CRC*

177. All 'relevant international treaties' under article 33 must be read alongside the requirements of the CRC. Here we consider this question with relation to the three international drug conventions. (The FCTC is far more explicit on the protection of 'minors')

178. The drug treaties and the CRC are all legally binding. But they operate concurrently, not in a vacuum.[299] Indeed, article 4 of the CRC refers to the 'framework of international co-operation', which could be read to include the international drug control system in the context of article 33. In addition, article 41 of the CRC states that 'nothing in the Convention shall affect any provisions which are more conducive to the realization of the rights of the child', in other words: the highest standard applies. But how should the CRC be read given the requirements of the drug treaties and what is the highest standard from a child rights perspective? How should the drug treaties be read in the light of the CRC, especially when there are gaps or omissions in those treaties?

179. We have already seen two ways in which the CRC may be read in the light of the drug treaties: defining which substances are involved and what qualifies as an illicit use; and representing the current international consensus on the broad controls to be applied to those substances (i.e. State practice). A third role, however, is that they represent, alongside article 33 itself, international consensus on a 'legitimate aim' for the purposes of assessing the proportionality of restrictions on certain rights—i.e. the protection of health and welfare.[300] But legitimate aim, of course, is not enough

---

[298] On this subject see S. Rolles *After the War on Drugs: Blueprint for Regulation* Transform Drug Policy Foundation, 2010; and S. Rolles 'An alternative to the war on drugs' *British Medical Journal* (2010) 341, c3360 doi: 10.1136/bmj.c3360 (Published 13 July 2010).

[299] Report of the Study Group of the International Law Commission, finalized by Martti Koskenniemi, *Fragmentation of International Law: Difficulties arising from the diversification and expansion of international law*, (UN Doc No A/CN.4/L.682, 2006), para. 120.

[300] The preamble of the 1961 Single Convention notes States parties concern for 'the health and welfare of mankind'. See, however, Air Canada v. UK, 5 May 1995, European Court of Human Rights, Application No. 18465/91, involving confiscation of property. The Court held that the confiscation of an airplane pending the payment of a fine was in 'the general interest in combating international drug trafficking', para. 42. The Court appears to have confused means and ends. Combating trafficking is a means to an end, not an end in itself.

in such analyses. Such measures must also be necessary in a democratic society for the achievement of that aim if rights restrictions are to be permissible. But that question has never been properly applied to the system of prohibition.[301] Similarly, the provisions of the drug conventions themselves have not been passed through a human rights filter, despite the fact that human rights were not a consideration in their drafting.[302] In other words, we must ask what a child rights analysis means for State practice moving forward.

180. It is to this issue that we now turn. When it comes to children, the drug treaties must be read in the light of the CRC to ensure appropriate interpretation.[303] This is supported by the status of human rights in the UN system,[304] the fact that the CRC contains *jus cogens* norms such as freedom from torture, and the repeated resolutions of the General Assembly that affirm that drug control must be carried out in full conformity with human rights. The reverse would be anathema to the role of human rights as a check and balance against the impact of law and policy on individuals and groups.

---

[301] See for example Prince v South Africa (Communication No. 1474/2006, UN Doc No CCPR/C/91/D/1474/2006, 2006) which appears to avoid in depth analyses of proportionality and in which the Committee found against Prince—a lawyer who was not permitted access to the bar on the basis of his religious drug use. Contrast this with the same case in the Constitutional Court of South Africa, where Ngcobo J delivered the dissenting view, finding in favour of Prince on the basis of an analysis of proportionality. The majority avoided this analysis and found in favour of the Law Society. (Prince v President of the Law Society of the Cape of Good Hope (CCT36/00) [2002] ZACC 1; 2002 (2) SA 794; 2002 (3) BCLR 231 (25 January 2002)).

[302] The official commentaries to the drug treaties are testament to this. See also William B. McAllister *Drug diplomacy in the twentieth century: an international history*, (New York, Routledge, 2000).

[303] They must also be read subject to other human rights treaties and relevant custom. See D. Barrett and M. Nowak 'The United Nations and Drug Policy: Towards a Human Rights-Based Approach' in *The Diversity Of International Law: Essays In Honour Of Professor Kalliopi K. Koufa*, Aristotle Constantinides and Nikos Zaikos, eds, (Amsterdam: Brill/Martinus Nijhoff), 2009 pp. 461–465.

[304] Human rights are considered one of the three pillars of the UN (see Manfred Nowak, 'The Three Pillars of the United Nations: Security, Development and Human Rights' in M. E. Salomon *et al.* (eds), *Casting the Net Wider: Human Rights, Development and New Duty-Bearers* (Antwerp/Oxford, Intersentia, 2007) 25–41. By contrast drug control is not referred to in the Charter, but was considered a sub-set of 'solutions of international economic, social, health, and related problems' under Article 55(1) of the Charter. See Fifth report of the Drafting Committee 11/3 of the San Francisco Conference, (WD 40 11/3/A/5, 25 May 1945); statements of the representatives of Canada, China, India and the United States in Committee 11/3, verbatim minutes of 19th meeting, 4 June 1945, cited in United Nations, *Commentary on the Single Convention on Narcotic Drugs 1961*, (New York, UN, 1973) p. 115.

This role for the CRC is vital for three main reasons:

1. The drug treaties are broadly framed and open to wide interpretation. There is significant 'room for manoeuvre'.[305]
2. The treaties contain provisions that explicitly permit States parties to take more severe measures than provided for in the treaties themselves.[306] These require human rights safeguards.
3. There are gaps in the drug conventions. As discussed above, children were not a focus in their drafting. These gaps must be filled by a child rights based interpretation of the drug conventions. Here, the concluding observations of the CRC Committee and human rights jurisprudence more broadly are helpful.

Let us consider some examples:

3.4.a Crop Eradication

181. Article 14(2) of the 1988 Convention Against the Illicit Traffic in Narcotic Drugs and Psychotropic Substances requires that States parties take 'appropriate measures to prevent illicit cultivation of and to eradicate plants containing narcotic or psychotropic substances'. Note the same qualifier as used in CRC article 33 'appropriate measures'. The article is also the only one in the three drug conventions to refer to human rights, stating that '[t]he measures adopted shall respect fundamental human rights'. From a child rights perspective the frame of reference and what must be considered *lex specialis* for what is appropriate in this regard is the CRC. With that in mind consider the following issues and related CRC provisions:

182. Aerial fumigation of coca in Colombia (the only country where currently this takes place) is known to result in harms to both physical and mental health, including of children and violates articles 6 and article 24. Tens of thousands of families have been displaced (articles 18, 24 and 27), including

---

[305] N. Dorn, and A. Jamieson, (eds) *European drug laws: the room for manoeuvre. The full report of a comparative legal research into drug laws of France, Germany, Italy, Spain, the Netherlands and Sweden and their relations to international drug conventions.* (Drugscope, London, 2001).

[306] Article 39 1961 Convention, article 23 1971 Convention, article 24 1988 Convention. In the official commentary on the 1961 convention the death penalty is identified as a 'permissible substitute control' for the purposes of the 1961 Convention (without making comment on the legality of the penalty on other grounds). *1961 Commentary* o.c. (note 305) pp. 449–450, para. 2.

indigenous people (article 30).[307] The former Special Rapporteur on the right to health, the former Special Rapporteur on the rights of indigenous people, the Working Group on the use of mercenaries and the Committee on the Rights of the Child have all raised concerns about this practice.[308] Those displaced by counter-narcotics measures are not entitled to social welfare (articles 26 and 39). This makes it extremely difficult to fully know the extent of displacement because of aerial fumigation, as there is every reason for families to conceal the reason they were forced to move.[309] Ecuador is currently suing Colombia before the International Court of Justice due to the effects of aerial spraying on its territory.[310]

183. Forced manual eradication, whereby teams tear up or plough fields by hand, is also problematic. In Colombia, for example, many farmers report theft of food, livestock and other provisions by the eradication teams (article 27). There have also been reports of sexual violence, plunder and houses burnt to the ground (article 19).[311]

184. The traditional use of coca for cultural and medicinal purposes in the Andean region is well known and well-established among indigenous groups. The 1961 Single Convention, article 49(2)(e), provided a 25 year grace period for coca chewing, which has now long expired. As such traditional uses of coca are not, it seems, permitted in international law, based on negotiations of treaties that entirely excluded indigenous people. Compare the view of James Anaya that '[i]t has become a generally accepted principle in international law that indigenous peoples should be consulted as to any

---

[307] For an overview see 'An exercise in futility: Nine years of fumigation in Colombia', Witness for Peace, Fundacion Minga and Institute for Policy Studies, 2007.

[308] Special Rapporteur on the right of everyone to the highest attainable standard of physical and metal health, Paul Hunt, Oral Remarks, 21 September 2007, Bogota, Colombia; Report of the Special Rapporteur on the situation of human rights and fundamental freedoms of indigenous people, Rodolfo Stavenhagen, Mission to Colombia, (UN Doc No E/CN.4/2005/88/Add.2, 2004) paras 46–52, & 106; Working Group on the question of the use of mercenaries as a means of violating human rights and impeding the exercise of the right of peoples to self-determination, Addendum: Mission to Ecuador, (UN Doc No A/HRC/4/42/Add.2, 2007) paras 47–51. Concluding Observations, Colombia, o.c. (note 112) para. 72.

[309] The non-governmental organisation CODHES estimates that there are over four million internally displaced people in Colombia. The Government estimates there to be closer to three million. UN Office for the Co-ordination of Humanitarian Affairs, Colombia humanitarian situation, synopsis; January–June 2009 (New York/Geneva, UN, 2009).

[310] International Court of Justice 'Ecuador institutes proceedings against Colombia with regard to a dispute concerning the alleged aerial spraying by Colombia of toxic herbicides over Ecuadorian territory' Press release No. 2008/5, 1 April 2008.

[311] Witness for Peace and Association Minga, Forced manual eradication: The wrong solution to the failed US counter-narcotics policy in Colombia, (Washington DC, September 2008).

decision affecting them'.[312] The now universally adopted Declaration on the Rights of Indigenous Peoples recognises this right[313] as well as the right of indigenous peoples to 'practise and revitalize their cultural traditions and customs'[314] 'to the use and control of their ceremonial objects'[315] 'to their traditional medicines'[316] 'to the lands, territories and resources which they have traditionally owned, occupied or otherwise used or acquired'[317] and 'to maintain, control, protect and develop their cultural heritage, traditional knowledge and traditional cultural expressions, as well as the manifestations of their sciences, technologies and cultures, including human and genetic resources, seeds, medicines, knowledge of the properties of fauna and flora'.[318] The UN Permanent Forum on Indigenous Issues (UN PFII) has recently supported the call for the removal of traditional uses of coca from the scope of international drug control.[319] According to the UN PFII in 2009, 'those portions of the [1961] Convention regarding coca leaf chewing that are inconsistent with the rights of indigenous peoples to maintain their traditional health and cultural practices, as recognized in articles 11, 24 and 31 of the Declaration, be amended and/or repealed'.[320] The blanket ban on traditional uses of such plants is an area of considerable conflict requiring

---

[312] 'Indigenous Peoples' Participatory Rights in Relation to Decisions about Natural Resource Extraction: The More Fundamental Issue of What Rights Indigenous Peoples Have in Land and Resources' *Arizona Journal of International and Comparative Law*, 1 (2005 (22)) 7.

[313] Article 18(1).

[314] Article 11(1).

[315] Article 12(1).

[316] Article 24(1).

[317] Article 26(1).

[318] Article 31(1).

[319] 'The Permanent Forum welcomes the decision 2009/250 of the Economic and Social Council on a proposed amendment to the Single Convention on Narcotic Drugs of 1961 as amended by the 1972 Protocol, related to the traditional use of the coca leaf. The Forum recommends that Member States support this initiative, taking into account articles 11, 24 and 31 of the United Nations Declaration on the Rights of Indigenous Peoples'. Report of the Ninth Session of the UN Permanent Forum on Indigenous Issues 19–30 April 2010, (UN Doc No E/2010/43–E/C.19/2010/15), para. 35.

[320] 'The Permanent Forum recognizes the cultural significance and medical importance of the coca leaf in the Andean and other indigenous regions of South America. It also notes that coca leaf chewing is specifically banned by the United Nations Single Convention on Narcotic Drugs (1961). The Permanent Forum recommends that those portions of the Convention regarding coca leaf chewing that are inconsistent with the rights of indigenous peoples to maintain their traditional health and cultural practices, as recognized in articles 11, 24 and 31 of the Declaration, be amended and/or repealed', Report of the Eighth Session of the UN Permanent Forum on Indigenous Issues 18–29 May 2009, (UN Doc No E/2009/43–E/C.19/2009/14), para. 89.

resolution and has recently led Bolivia to denounce the 1961 Single Convention. It will re-accede with a reservation on the relevant provision.[321]

185. Eradication campaigns in other countries have been shown to have negative impacts on family income (articles 18, 27), food security (articles 24, 27) and school enrolment (article 28).[322] In 2005, for example, the World Bank warned that, in Afghanistan, 'an abrupt shrinkage of the opium economy or falling opium prices without new means of livelihood would significantly worsen rural poverty'.[323] Crop eradication measures in Afghanistan have contributed to the practice of child bartering (selling) to pay opium debts[324] (articles 9, 19, 34 and the Optional Protocol to the CRC on the sale of children, child prostitution and child pornography).

186. In contributing to these various child rights problems, it must be questioned whether such measures may be deemed 'appropriate' from a child rights perspective. A child rights-based reading of article 14(2) of the 1988 Convention would require a more careful approach, and would instead favour consensual alternative development measures, properly sequenced (i.e. alternatives being in place prior to the eradication of illicit crops) and supported by adequate infrastructure to support the new industry. This in turn is supported by the 'Political Declaration and Plan of Action on International Cooperation Towards an Integrated and Balanced Strategy to Counter the World Drug Problem' adopted in 2009 at the High Level Segment of the 53rd Session of the UN Commission on Narcotic Drugs.[325] The plan of action highlighted the problem of 'ill-sequenced policy interventions'[326] and called on

---

[321] The formal denunciation is available at http://treaties.un.org/doc/Publication/CN/2011/CN.421.2011-Eng.pdf; See also 'Bolivia withdraws from the UN Single Convention on Narcotic Drugs' Transnational Institute, 30 June 2011 http://www.druglawreform.info/en/issues/unscheduling-the-coca-leaf/item/2593-bolivia-withdraws-from-the-un-single-convention-on-narcotic-drugs.

[322] See for example, 'Thematic Evaluation of UNODC's Alternative Development Initiatives', Independent Evaluation Unit of the UNODC, (Vienna, November 2005). 23–24; and M. Jelsma and T. Kramer, *Withdrawal Symptoms, Changes in the Southeast Asian Drugs Market*, (Amsterdam, Transnational Institute, August 2008). 18–19.

[323] The World Bank, *Afghanistan—State Building, Sustaining Growth and Reducing Poverty*, (Washington DC, 2005) A World Bank Country Report, 118–119.

[324] *Ahmadzai & C. Kuonqui* 'In the shadows of the insurgency in Afghanistan: Child bartering, opium debt and the war on drugs' in D. Barrett (ed.) *Children of the Drug War: Perspectives on the Impact of Drug Policies on Young People*, New York and Amsterdam, International Debate Education Association, iDebate Press, 2011.

[325] Economic and Social Council, 'Report of the 53rd session of the UN Commission on Narcotic Drugs 14 March 2008 and 11–20 March 2009, (UN Doc No E/2009/28—E/CN.7/2009/12).

[326] Ibid., para. 46.

member States to 'Develop alternative development programmes and eradication measures while fully respecting relevant international instruments, including human rights instruments'.[327]

3.4.b Drug Dependence Treatment

187. As noted above, articles 38 of the 1961 Convention and 20 of the 1971 Convention require States parties to put in place drug dependence treatment for those in need.[328] If this obligation is to have relevance to children, and if their rights are to be respected, protected and fulfilled, it must be read in the light of the CRC. As noted in June 2011 by the CRC Committee, States parties must 'Ensure that dependence, detoxification, treatment, rehabilitation and reintegration interventions of children using drugs comply with international human rights standards'.[329]

188. The Convention on the Rights of the Child imposes both positive and negative obligations on States parties. Looking at positive obligations, for example, article 24 would require that any such treatment measures be available, accessible, acceptable and of sufficient quality.[330] This, in turn, would demand that they be suited to the specific needs of children and young people and based on scientific evidence and best practice. Moreover, drug dependence does not often exist in isolation from other issues, including for, example, mental health (co-morbidity). As such, appropriate psychological evaluations are important. Adopting a holistic approach and recognising the inter-relatedness of rights may help provide a legal framework for addressing such complexities.

189. When engaging the negative obligations, the treatment must not result in abuses of the rights of the child. This should go without saying, but there are in fact many examples of children being abused in the name of drug treatment—being detained arbitrarily, forced to work and subjected to various forms of cruel inhuman and degrading treatment.[331] These measures would of course violate numerous articles in the Convention, but are not necessarily prohibited by the drug treaties if read in isolation due to the

---

[327] Ibid., para. 47(b).
[328] The then outgoing Executive Director of the UN Office on Drugs and Crime, Antonio Maria Costa, stressed this in his foreword to the *World Drug Report 2010*. See *World Drug Report 2010*, (UN Office On Drugs and Crime, Vienna, 2010) p. 4.
[329] *Concluding Observations: Cambodia* o.c. (note 68).
[330] General Comment No. 14 o.c. (note 61), para. 12.
[331] See, for example, *Skin on the Cable* o.c. (note 25).

absence of human rights norms within their provisions. Article 25 (child's right to periodic review of treatment)[332] aims to address this type of situation by preventing the continuation of an undesired situation, while article 37 (reflecting a norm of *jus cogens*) strictly prohibits torture or cruel inhuman or degrading treatment or punishment.

3.4.c   Harm Reduction

190. Harm reduction is an area of practice, science and policy that has been proven to reduce the health and social harms of drug use. However, harm reduction has until recently received little attention in international law, or in the recommendations of the Committee on the Rights of the Child (as it relates to children and young people). Both the drug conventions and the CRC are silent on harm reduction. This is inevitable, as harm reduction as policy and practice has really only emerged in the last two decades, mostly in the field of HIV prevention.

191. Whether harm reduction is permitted under the drug conventions remains contested, albeit by a small minority.[333] The International Narcotics Control Board weakly supports aspects of harm reduction such as needle and syringe programmes and opioid substitution therapy,[334] but is antagonistic towards others such as safer crack kits (to help reduce the health harms associated with crack smoking) and safe consumption rooms (where people can use drugs under medical supervision).[335] The Board considers the latter two to be in breach the drug conventions, although there is little in the way of legal argument to support this.[336] State practice, as increasing numbers employ harm reduction measures, points in the other direction. The best that can be said is that harm reduction is discretionary under the drug conventions. Banning harm reduction is not prohibited.

---

[332] Which itself should now be read in conjunction with the *UN Principles for the protection of persons with mental illness and the improvement of mental health care*' (UN Doc No GA/RES/46/119, 1991) *Annex.*

[333] See Alison Crocket, 'The Function and Relevance of the Commission in Narcotic Drugs in the pursuit of Humane Drug Policy (or the ramblings of a bewildered diplomat'), *International Journal on Human Rights and Drug Policy*, vol. 1, 2010, pp. 83–90.

[334] See, for example, International Narcotics Control Board, *Report of the International Narcotics Control Board for 1993*, (UN Doc NoE/INCB/1993/1), ch. 1.

[335] International Narcotics Control Board, *Report of the International Narcotics Control Board for 2009*, (UN Doc NoE/INCB/2009/1), para. 278.

[336] See UN Drug Control Programme Legal Affairs Section, 'Flexibility of Treaty Provisions as Regards Harm Reduction Approaches'(UN Doc NoE/INCB/2002/W.13/SS.5, 2002) (Restricted). This advice was requested by the INCB but aspects of it ignored. See paras. 21–28 on safe injection rooms.

192. While most drug use among young people does not lead to significant health harms, especially risky behaviour such as injecting drug use is a serious problem among children in some countries. The age of initiation into drug use and injecting drug use is frequently below eighteen, and in some countries the age is decreasing. The first years of injecting are particularly risky, requiring early intervention.[337] The evidence base for the effectiveness of harm reduction in addressing the harms of such use (such as HIV transmission, overdose, abscesses etc) is very strong.[338] But despite this in many countries where harm reduction services are available,[339] age restrictions are applied to them, excluding by law those under a certain age. There are many examples, but sixteen and eighteen tend to be common cut-off points. Some countries apply higher restrictions.[340] Age, of course, is an important factor in deciding treatment options and interventions. Methadone, for example, would be a rare intervention for a very young opiate user. But it is an issue of risk assessment, the appropriateness of certain treatments, and the threshold of intervention. Age should not be a criterion of exclusion. Decisions must be taken in the best interests of the child (article 3), and with due regard for their evolving capacities (article 5), their development (article 6) and their right to be heard (article 12).

193. That harm reduction may now be a recognised requirement of the right to health of people who use drugs is becoming clear. This has been supported by the current and former Special Rapporteurs on the right to health,[341] by the Human Rights Council[342] and consistently by the CESCR Committee.[343] In

---

[337] *Young people and injecting drug use in selected countries of Central and Eastern Europe*, o.c. (note 13).

[338] R. Jürgens et al., People who use drugs, HIV and human rights, *The Lancet* (2010 (376)) 9739, 475-5485; C. Beyer et al., Time to act: a call for comprehensive responses to HIV in people who use drugs, *The Lancet*, (2010 (376)) 9740, 551–563.

[339] There are now eighty-two countries worldwide where needle and syringe programmes are operating. C. Cook (ed.) 'Global State of Harm Reduction 2010: Key issues for broadening the response' (London: Harm Reduction International, 20100.

[340] See for example the Swedish Lag (2006:323) *om utbyte av sprutor och kanyler* (Legislation (2006: 323) *on exchange of needles and cannulas*) which restricts access to needle and syringe programmes to those over twenty.

[341] Report of the Special Rapporteur on the right of everyone to the enjoyment of the highest attainable standard of physical and mental health, Paul Hunt: *Mission to Sweden* (UN Doc No A/HRC/4/28/Add.2, 2007) para. 60.; Report of the Special Rapporteur on the right of everyone to the enjoyment of the highest attainable standard of physical and mental health, Anand Grover (UN Doc No A/65/255, 2010) paras. 50–61.

[342] Human Rights Council resolution 12/27, *The protection of human rights in the context of human immunodeficiency virus (HIV) and acquired immunodeficiency syndrome (AIDS)* (UN Doc No A/HRC/RES/12/27, 2009) para. 5.

[343] O.c. (note 103).

2010, that Committee explicitly called for youth focused harm reduction, and connected it also to the right to benefit from scientific progress and its applications. The Committee called on Mauritius to, 'Remove age barriers to accessing opioid substitution therapy and develop youth-friendly harm reduction services tailored to the specific needs of young people who use drugs.'[344] In its General Comment on HIV/AIDS cited above, the CRC Committee appears to support this conclusion. In 2009, the Committee also recommended that Sweden ensure 'the provision of necessary evidence-based support, recovery and reintegration services to all children affected by substance abuse ... aimed at effectively reducing the harmful consequences of such abuse'.[345] Most recently, the Committee in 2011 explicitly called for 'specialised and youth-friendly drug dependence treatment and harm reduction services for children and young people'.[346] While harm reduction for children and young people may be optional under the drug conventions, it may be also an obligation under the Convention on the Rights of the Child and Covenant on Economic, Social and Cultural Rights. But far more work is needed on what safe, effective and rights based harm reduction for young people looks like in practice, including, crucially, in relation to recreational drug use.

3.4.d   *Access to Essential Controlled Medicines*

194. Some drug use is beneficial. The drug conventions contain dual obligations to reduce supply and demand for illicit purposes and to ensure access to drugs for medical and scientific purposes. The International Narcotics Control Board operates an estimates system under the 1961 Convention whereby States parties must report on controlled drugs required for medical and scientific purposes to ensure that adequate quantities are imported.[347] This is vital given that the 1961 Convention covers drugs such as morphine. Approximately 80% of the world's population has insufficient access, or no access at all, to opiates for pain relief.[348] This includes millions of children in need of palliative care. It is an issue that is inseparable from drug use and measures to address the illicit drug trade because overly restrictive narcotics laws and 'scare messages' about these drugs are known to contribute

---

[344] O.c. (note 62), para. 27(c).
[345] *Concluding Observations: Sweden*, 2009 o.c. (note 35) para. 49.
[346] *Concluding Observations: Ukraine*, o.c. (note 63) para. 60(a).
[347] Single Convention 1961 o.c. (note 4) Articles, 12, 19.
[348] Mary Ann Overland, 'Morphine Remains Scarce for pain Sufferers Worldwide', *Time*, 7 June 2010.

to the lack of access to such medicines for children in need.[349] It should be recalled that article 33 protects children from 'illicit' use.

195. It is clear that the obligation to ensure availability of opiates for medical purposes is considerably weaker than those relating to restricting access for recreational uses. Its strongest affirmation found in the 1961 Convention is in the preamble, and therefore not binding (although it does provide important context for the purpose and importance of the estimates system and the protection of medical uses).[350] The 1971 Convention merely states that access to psychotropic substances for medical purposes should not be unduly restricted.[351] This is an issue the INCB has taken up, however, reasserting this obligation.[352]

196. A child rights-based analysis, taking into account the best interests of the child (in this case children in need of such medicines), the right to life survival and development, the right to health, and freedom from cruel, inhuman and degrading treatment would serve to strengthen the obligation to ensure the availability of opiates for palliative care.[353] Indeed, in 2011, the Committee on the Rights of the Child recognised that palliative care for children is related to articles 6 and 24 of the Convention, and recommended that Belarus 'establish a funding mechanism for the provision of palliative care for children and support the palliative care services provided by non-governmental organizations'.[354] While the Committee has yet to address the issue of access to essential medicines for palliative care specifically, it would appear sensible that the Convention requires that laws and policies aimed at addressing recreational use and drug trafficking do not impede access to essential medicines for children.

197. Each of these areas requires further study, as do others not covered here relating to other aspects of drug control. In particular, what do article

---

[349] For example, Human Rights Watch, *Needless pain: Government failure to provide palliative care for children in Kenya*, (New York, Human Rights Watch, 2010), which includes a description of the 'chilling effect' of narcotics laws on access to controlled medicines for pain relief.

[350] Ibid., preamble. 'Recognizing that the medical use of narcotic drugs continues to be indispensable for the relief of pain and suffering and that adequate provision must be made to ensure the availability of narcotic drugs for such purposes.'

[351] 1971 Convention o.c. (note 4) preamble.

[352] International Narcotics Control Board, *Report of the International Narcotics Control Board for 1999*, (UN Doc No E/INCB/1999/1, 1999), ch. 1.

[353] Diederik Lohman, Rebecca Schleifer and Joseph Amon, 'Access to pain treatment as a human right' *BMC Medicine*, vol. 8: 8, 20 January 2010.

[354] Committee on the Rights of the Child, *Concluding Observations: Belarus*, (UN Doc No CRC/C/DNK/4, 2011), para. 56.

40 of the Convention on the Rights of the Child and juvenile justice standards have to say about the penal provisions of the drug conventions in the context of children who are drug dependent? Article 3 of the 1988 Convention requires the criminalisation of possession of controlled drugs for personal use subject to constitutional limitations. What does this mean for countries where the Convention on the Rights of the Child or child rights provisions based on it have been incorporated into the national constitution or those in legal systems whereby international treaties are incorporated into national law? Is the criminal law an appropriate basis for addressing drug use among children? There is room for decriminalisation in the drug conventions. The INCB has been inconsistent in its view on this, accepting it in Portugal but criticising constitutional decisions elsewhere.[355] This is a very important discussion given the number of children who come into contact with the criminal justice system due to drug use and drug related crime.[356]

---

[355] Contrast the Board's view on Portugal (International Narcotics Control Board, *Report of the International Narcotics Control Board for 2004*, (UN Doc NoE/INCB/2004/1, 2005, para. 538) with its views on Argentina, Brazil and Mexico (International Narcotics Control Board, *Report of the International Narcotics Control Board for 2009*, UN Doc No E/INCB/2009/1, 2010, para. 453.)

[356] See, for example, *Young people and injecting drug use in selected countries of Central and Eastern Europe*, o.c. (note 13).

CONCLUSION

198. The issues of children and young people who use drugs, parental drug use, and children's involvement in the drug trade are many and extremely complex. No one paper can do justice to these complexities. But our analysis of article 33 of the CRC may be summarised with the following five broad conclusions:

There Are Two Substantive Protections in Article 33

a. Appropriate measures, including legislative, administrative, social and educational measures, to protect children from the illicit use of narcotic drugs and psychotropic substances as defined in the relevant international treaties. This involves not just one level of protection (i.e. primary prevention) but four:
   - Reduction of initiation
   - Protection of children currently using drugs (recreationally, problematically etc.)
   - Protection from drug use in the family (especially parental drug use)
   - Protection from drug use in the community

b. Appropriate measures, including legislative, administrative, social and educational measures, to prevent the use of children in the illicit production and traffic of narcotic drugs and psychotropic substances as defined in the relevant international treaties.

'Appropriateness' frames both substantive protections and itself may be broken down into a series of five broad principles.

Appropriate measures must be:

   - Read alongside the remaining articles of the CRC (in particular the General Principles)
   - Read in the light of other provisions of international law which provide greater protection
   - Address patterns of vulnerability including a gender perspective

- Evidence-based (i.e. not arbitrary)
- Proportionate

The 'relevant international treaties' play what may be called a 'subjective' role (describing the substances captured by the article), rather than a normative one (determining what measures are 'appropriate' for the purposes of article 33).

'Relevant international treaties', as they apply to children, must be read alongside the CRC

The relationship between the CRC and 'other relevant treaties' indicates that the CRC is open in terms of the larger policy paradigm adopted to 'protect' children or define 'illicit' use, production and trafficking.

199. In these broad conclusions we find a basis for further study and discussion on article 33, drug use, and the involvement of children in the drug trade. They also relate to the interpretation of international law and provide a framework for scrutinising national laws and policies in this field from a child rights perspective.

200. Since the CRC was drafted we know much more about risk factors for drug use, dependence and drug related harms. We know more about what is effective and ineffective in terms of prevention, treatment and harm reduction, and which groups of children are more at risk and why. We know more about children's involvement in the drug trade and the myriad factors contributing to this phenomenon. And we know much more about child rights based approaches to multiple social issues. Still, not enough attention has been paid to articulating a child rights based approach to drug policies and to the many issues children face in relation to drugs and the drug trade. This is true of the CRC Committee, governments and civil society organisations. It is time now to take child rights more seriously in drug control, and drug control more seriously in child rights.